T H E   B O O K   O F

VEGETARIAN
COOKING

T H E   B O O K   O F

VEGETARIAN
COOKING

LOUISE PICKFORD

Photographed by
JON STEWART

HPBooks
a division of
PRICE STERN SLOAN
Los Angeles

ANOTHER BEST SELLING VOLUME FROM HPBOOKS

HPBooks
A division of Price Stern Sloan, Inc.
11150 Olympic Boulevard
Suite 650
Los Angeles, California 90064

9 8 7 6 5 4 3 2 1

By arrangement with Salamander Books Ltd.

© Salamander Books Ltd., 1993

Library of Congress Cataloging-in-Publication Data
Pickford, Louise
      The book of vegetarian cooking/Louise Pickford.
         p.   cm.
      Includes index.
      ISBN 1-55788-076-X
      1. Vegetarian cookery.   I. Title
TX837.P5284   1993
641.5'636—dc20   93-24642
                                                            CIP

Home Economists: Kerenza Harries and Jo Craig
Printed in Belgium by Proost International Book Production

CONTENTS

INTRODUCTION

With the emphasis on a more healthy lifestyle, vegetarian cooking is fast becoming the most attractive way of providing a highly nutritious and versatile diet. *The Book of Vegetarian Cooking* is a delicious collection of recipes based on unusual combinations of fresh vegetables, fruits, pasta, rice, grains, eggs and cheeses, with recipes for both vegetarians and vegans, as well as those who simply enjoy meatless dishes.

Lowfat alternatives to cream and cheese are given in many of the recipes, and butter is only suggested where it is essential for the flavor of the dish. However, there are some rich and creamy dishes as well for those who enjoy the occasional indulgence.

The recipes are chosen from all parts of the world to give a truly international selection. Divided into nine sections, this book offers a wide choice of recipes, ranging from warming winter soups and elegant appetizers, light brunches and suppers and sensational salads, to elegant dinner party dishes and delicious desserts.

With over 100 recipes, each one illustrated in full color and with step-by-step directions, this is the essential book for vegetarians who want to enjoy a varied diet. By planning your meals from the recipes in this book, you will be able to ensure a well-balanced and healthy diet, with food that is fun to cook and delicious to eat.

THE VEGETARIAN DIET

A well-balanced diet is essential for healthy living. It is generally accepted that we should all eat less fat, sugar and salt and more cereals, starchy foods, vitamins and minerals. By excluding meat in your diet, you can decrease your fat intake, but do not replace meat with too much high-fat dairy products, with the misguided notion of only replacing protein.

Many staple foods, such as nuts, breads, soy products and brown rice, contain high proportions of protein. Essential minerals and vitamins are present in many fresh vegetables, and by eating starchy foods, particularly rice, pasta and bread, you can get a good supply of complex carbohydrates.

The following are some of the ingredients used that may be unfamiliar.

Balsamic vinegar: An Italian vinegar aged in barrels. It is dark in color with a slightly sweet flavor.

Creamed coconut: Sold in blocks, this flavors and thickens sauces, but it should only be used in small amounts. It will separate if allowed to boil.

Crème fraîche: A thick cream similar to sour cream, which will not separate when cooked at a high temperature.

Dried ceps: Dried mushrooms also known as porcini; these have an intense flavor and are used in small amounts. Reconstitute in boiling water before using.

Grated horseradish: Freshly grated horseradish is available in jars. Alternatively, use creamed horseradish.

Kirsch: A cherry flavored liqueur.

Lemon grass: A hard grass used in Far Eastern cooking, this has a fragrant lemon flavor and should be lightly crushed to allow flavors to escape. Available from ethnic stores.

Mascarpone: An Italian fresh cream cheese, with a light texture and natural sweet flavor.

Mushrooms: When a recipe calls for mixed mushrooms, use any different fresh varieties available, such as field, ceps, oyster and shiitake.

Pecorino: An Italian semihard cheese with a flavor similar to Parmesan.

Polenta: A coarse grained cornmeal.

Puy lentils: Small blue-brown lentils, with a delicious nutty flavor; brown or green lentils may be used instead.

Sechuan peppers: Highly aromatic reddish-brown peppercorns used in Oriental cooking

Sun-dried tomatoes: Dried tomatoes which are sold either in packages and need to be reconstituted in boiling water, or in oil, when they simply need to be drained. They have an intensely sweet tomato flavor, and should only be used in small quantities. Sun-dried tomato paste is also available.

Tamarind paste: Made from the bean-like fruit of the tamarind tree, the paste has a lemony flavor.

OTHER INGREDIENTS

Butter should be unsalted wherever possible; substitute vegetable margarine or oil, if wished.

Vegetable stock should be home-made if possible; see the recipe on page 65, or blend good-quality stock cubes with vegetable cooking water.

Olive oil, if used raw, should always be virgin. A lesser-quality oil can be used for frying, broiling, grilling and roasting.

Sea salt should be used when possible, and pepper should always be freshly ground black peppercorns unless otherwise stated.

HIDDEN DANGERS

Strict vegetarians should be careful to check packages before purchasing products. The foods that may contain animal products are cheeses – many of the recipes state a particular vegetarian cheese – and bottled sauces.

ITALIAN BEAN SOUP

1 cup dried borlotti beans, soaked overnight in cold
    water to cover
1 bay leaf and 1 sprig each thyme and rosemary
5 cups vegetable stock (page 65)
2 tablespoons olive oil
1 onion, chopped
1 garlic clove, chopped
1 teaspoon each chopped fresh rosemary, sage and
    thyme
2 carrots, chopped
2 celery stalks, chopped
1 large zucchini, chopped
1/3 cup dry red wine
1-1/4 cups tomato juice
2 tablespoons chopped fresh parsley
Salt and pepper

Drain beans. Into a large pan, place beans
with bay leaf, thyme and rosemary. Add
stock. Bring to a boil and boil 10 minutes.
Reduce heat, cover and simmer 45 to 50
minutes or until beans are tender. In a skillet,
heat oil. Add onion, garlic, chopped herbs,
carrots, celery and zucchini and cook 5
minutes. Add wine. Boil rapidly 3 minutes.
Add tomato juice. Cover and simmer 20
minutes.

Drain cooked beans, reserving liquid. In a
blender or food processor, puree half the
beans with 2/3 cup of the liquid. Stir into
vegetable mixture. Stir in remaining beans,
3-3/4 cups of the liquid, the parsley, salt and
pepper. Bring to a boil and cook 5 minutes.

Makes 8 servings.

– MUSHROOM & BARLEY BROTH –

1/3 cup barley, soaked overnight in cold water to cover
4-1/2 cups vegetable stock (page 65)
1/4 cup dried cep mushrooms
2/3 cup boiling water
3 tablespoons olive oil
3 shallots, finely chopped
2 teaspoons chopped fresh thyme
5 cups sliced mixed fresh mushrooms
2/3 cup hard cider
1 bay leaf
1 teaspoon Dijon-style mustard
Salt and pepper

Drain barley. Into a large pan, place barley and add stock. Bring to a boil, then reduce heat, cover and simmer 45 minutes. Soak dried ceps in boiling water 20 minutes. Drain ceps, reserving liquid, and chop.

In a large pan, heat oil. Add shallots and thyme; cook 5 minutes. Add ceps and fresh mushrooms. Stir-fry over medium heat 5 minutes or until golden. Add cider and boil rapidly until liquid is almost evaporated. Add barley with stock, reserved cep liquid, bay leaf and mustard to pan. Simmer, covered, 15 minutes. Season with salt and pepper and serve with whole-wheat rolls.

Makes 6 to 8 servings.

TOMATO, OLIVE & BREAD SOUP

2 pounds very ripe tomatoes
3 tablespoons olive oil
1 onion, chopped
2 garlic cloves, crushed
4 slices day-old Italian bread, cubed
1 tablespoon chopped fresh sage
2/3 cup dry white wine
2-1/2 cups vegetable stock (page 65)
1 tablespoon tomato paste
1 teaspoon balsamic vinegar
1/2 cup pitted ripe olives, finely chopped
1 tablespoon finely grated Parmesan cheese

Peel and seed tomatoes over a bowl to catch any juices and finely chop flesh; set aside. In a large saucepan, heat oil. Add onion, garlic, bread and sage; stir-fry over medium heat 5 minutes or until bread is golden.

Add wine to pan. Boil until almost evaporated, then stir in tomatoes with any juices, stock, tomato paste and vinegar. Bring to a boil, reduce heat, cover and simmer 15 minutes. Blend olives and cheese together and use to garnish soup.

Makes 6 servings.

——CELERIAC & CHEESE SOUP——

2 tablespoons butter or margarine
1 onion, chopped
2-2/3 cups cubed peeled celeriac
2/3 cup hard cider
3-1/4 cups vegetable stock (page 65)
1 tablespoon chopped fresh parsley
2 small red apples, quartered
1 tablespoon olive oil
2 ounces vegetarian blue cheese, crumbled
1 tablespoon snipped fresh chives
Salt and pepper
Parsley sprigs, to garnish

In a large pan, melt butter. Add onion and celeriac; cook 6 to 8 minutes or until light golden. Add cider. Boil rapidly 3 minutes. Add stock and parsley, reduce heat, cover and simmer 20 minutes. Meanwhile preheat broiler.

Arrange apple slices on a baking sheet; brush with a little oil. Broil 1 to 2 minutes on each side or until lightly charred. Reserve 6 to 8 slices for garnish and add remainder to soup. Cook 3 to 4 minutes longer, then puree soup and the cheese in a blender or food processor until smooth. Return to pan. Stir in chives, salt and pepper; heat through. Transfer to warmed soup bowls, garnish with reserved apples and parsley sprigs and serve hot.

Makes 6 to 8 servings.

── CURRIED COCONUT SOUP ──

2 tablespoons olive oil
1 onion, chopped
1 garlic clove, crushed
1 teaspoon grated peeled gingerroot
2 teaspoons curry powder
1/2 cup long-grain white rice
5 cups vegetable stock (page 65)
6 ounces spinach
2 ounces creamed coconut
2/3 cup boiling water
1 tablespoon chopped fresh cilantro
Salt and pepper

In a large saucepan, heat oil. Add onion, garlic, gingerroot and curry powder.

Cook 5 minutes, add rice. Stir-fry 2 minutes or until transparent. Add stock. Bring to a boil, reduce heat, cover and simmer 10 minutes. Rinse spinach, discard tough stems and dry well. Cut into thin shreds. Add to pan and cook 5 minutes longer.

Into a small bowl, place coconut. Stir in boiling water, stirring until melted. Stir into pan with cilantro. Heat through 2 to 3 minutes, without boiling. Taste and adjust seasoning. Serve hot.

Makes 6 to 8 servings.

—EGGPLANT & GARLIC SOUP—

2 eggplants, peeled
4 tablespoons olive oil
4 garlic cloves, peeled
1/4 cup water
1 onion, chopped
1 zucchini, chopped
2 tomatoes, peeled, seeded and diced
1 teaspoon chopped fresh thyme
2 teaspoons lemon juice
3-3/4 cups vegetable stock (page 65)
Salt and pepper
Diced peeled tomatoes, grated lemon zest and thyme
   leaves, to garnish

Preheat broiler. With a sharp knife, cut eggplants lengthwise into 1/4-inch slices. Brush
with a little oil. Place on a baking sheet. Broil
until lightly charred, then turn over and broil
other sides until lightly charred. In a skillet,
heat 1 tablespoon oil over low heat. Add
garlic; cook 5 minutes or until golden, then
add water. Cover and simmer 5 minutes until
soft. Using a fork, mash.

In a large saucepan, heat remaining oil. Add
onion; cook 3 minutes or until soft. Add
zucchini, tomatoes and thyme. Cook 3
minutes. Add eggplants, mashed garlic,
lemon juice and stock. Bring to a boil, then
cover and simmer 15 minutes. In a blender or
food processor, puree soup until smooth.
Return to pan. Season to taste and heat
through, 5 minutes. Garnish and serve hot.

Makes 6 servings.

—SPICED BLACK BEAN SOUP—

1-1/2 cups dried black beans, soaked, overnight in cold
  water to cover
2 tablespoons olive oil
1 onion, chopped
1 garlic clove, chopped
1 dried red chile, seeded and chopped
2 carrots, chopped
1 celery stalk, chopped
5 cups vegetable stock (page 65)
1 teaspoon each toasted coriander seeds, cumin seeds
  and allspice berries
1 bay leaf
1/2 cup unsalted butter, softened
Grated peel and juice of 1/2 lime
1 tablespoon chopped fresh cilantro
Salt and pepper

Drain beans; rinse well. In a large saucepan, heat oil. Add onion, garlic, chile, carrots and celery; cook, stirring, 5 minutes or until browned. Add beans and stock. Slowly bring to a boil. Boil 10 minutes. Tie spices and bay leaf in a small piece of cheesecloth. Add to pan. Cover and simmer 1 to 1-1/4 hours or until beans are tender. Discard cheesecloth bag.

Meanwhile, prepare lime butter. Cream together butter, lime peel, lime juice, chopped cilantro, salt and pepper. Roll into a log shape. Refrigerate until required. To serve, cut log into 12 to 16 slices. In a blender, puree soup. Spoon into bowls and serve topped with 2 slices of lime butter.

Makes 6 to 8 servings.

Note: For vegans, omit the lime butter.

——FRAGRANT THAI BROTH——

3-3/4 cups vegetable stock (page 65)
2 gingerroot slices
2 cilantro sprigs
1 stem lemon grass, lightly crushed
1 red chile
1 garlic clove, crushed
1 cup diced plain tofu
2 tablespoons light soy sauce
2 ounces dried whole-wheat noodles
2 carrots, cut into matchstick pieces
1-1/4 cups sliced shiitake mushrooms
2 teaspoons tamarind paste or lemon juice
Cilantro leaves, to garnish

Into a large pan, pour stock. Add gingerroot, cilantro sprigs, lemon grass, chile and garlic. Slowly bring to a boil. Cover and simmer 25 minutes. Meanwhile, marinate tofu in soy sauce 25 minutes.

In a large pan of boiling water, cook noodles according to package directions. Drain well and transfer to warmed soup bowls. Into a clean pan, strain stock. Add soy sauce and tofu, carrots and mushrooms. Simmer 2 to 3 minutes until tender. Arrange tofu and vegetables over noodles. Beat tamarind paste or lemon juice into stock. Return to a boil and pour over noodles. Garnish with cilantro leaves and serve at once.

Makes 4 servings.

TOFU, LEEK & MUSHROOM SATE

3/4 pound plain tofu
3 leeks, trimmed
12 shiitake or button mushrooms
2 tablespoons dark soy sauce
1 garlic clove, crushed
1/2 teaspoon grated fresh gingerroot
1 small red chile, seeded and chopped
Grated peel and juice of 1 lime
3 tablespoons sweet sherry
2 teaspoons honey
1/4 cup crunchy peanut butter
1 ounce creamed coconut

With a sharp knife, cut tofu into 12 cubes and leeks into 12 thick slices. Place in a shallow dish with mushrooms. Mix together soy sauce, garlic, gingerroot, chile, lime peel, lime juice, sherry, honey and 3 tablespoons water. Pour over tofu mixture. Cover and refrigerate several hours, stirring from time to time.

Onto 8 bamboo skewers, thread the tofu, leeks and mushrooms. In a small pan, put 2/3 cup of the marinade. Add peanut butter and coconut. Heat gently until melted, then stir until thickened. Brush sauce over skewers. Place in a baking pan. Pour remaining marinade over and broil 10 to 12 minutes, turning and brushing with pan juices, until golden and lightly charred. Serve with sauce as a dip.

Makes 4 servings.

—TOFU WITH TOMATO SALSA—

3/4 pound smoked tofu
TOMATO SALSA:
1 large, ripe beef tomato, peeled, seeded and diced
2 sun-dried tomatoes in oil, drained and chopped
1 small garlic clove, chopped
1 tablespoon chopped fresh parsley
1 tablespoon shredded fresh basil
1 small red chile, seeded and finely chopped
1 teaspoon red-wine vinegar
1/4 teaspoon sugar
1/4 cup olive oil
Salt and freshly ground pepper

Drain tofu. Pat dry and, with a sharp knife, cut into 12 thin slices. Into a shallow dish, place tofu. To prepare salsa: In a bowl, combine fresh and dried tomatoes, garlic, herbs, chili pepper, vinegar and sugar. Beat in oil.

Spoon tomato mixture over sliced tofu. Cover and marinate 30 minutes. Arrange on serving plates, spooning all juices over tofu. Sprinkle with a little salt and plenty of pepper.

Makes 6 servings.

— MARINATED MOZZARELLA —

6 large garlic cloves, unpeeled
2 cups virgin olive oil
1 teaspoon cilantro seeds
1 teaspoon fennel seeds
1/2 teaspoon black peppercorns
14 ounces mozzarella cheese
2 dried red chiles
2 lemon peel strips
1 rosemary sprig, bruised
1 thyme sprig, bruised
1/4 cup ripe or green olives
Nectarine slices and mint sprigs, to garnish

In a pan of cold water, place garlic cloves. Simmer 15 minutes. Drain well and pat dry.

In a small skillet, heat 1 tablespoon of the oil over medium heat. Add garlic; cook 8 to 10 minutes or until golden and softened. Remove with a slotted spoon and drain on paper towels. In a heavy skillet, dry-fry spice seeds and peppercorns 1 to 2 minutes or until browned; cool.

Cut mozzarella cheese into bite-size pieces. In a large jar, layer cheese with garlic, fried spices, chiles, lemon peel, herbs and olives. Add enough oil to cover. Seal jar. Marinate several days in a cool place, but not the refrigerator, to allow time for flavors to develop. Serve cheese and garlic cloves with a slice of fresh bread, garnished with nectarine slices and mint sprigs.

Makes 6 servings.

—— BROILED GRAPE LEAVES ——

4 green onions, finely chopped
1 small nectarine or peach, finely chopped
1 tablespoon chopped fresh mint
1/4 teaspoon ground coriander
Pinch of ground cumin
Salt and pepper
4 ounces goat cheese
8 large grape leaves in brine, drained
Olive oil, for brushing

In a small bowl, place onions, nectarine or peach, mint and spices. Season with salt and pepper and stir until combined. Cut cheese into 4 equal slices.

Rinse and dry grape leaves. Arrange in pairs, overlapping, and brush leaf tops with oil. Place 1 slice of cheese at one end of each 2 leaves. Top with the nectarine mixture. Carefully fold leaves over the cheese until completely covered. Secure with wooden picks.

Preheat broiler. Brush leaf packages with oil. Place on a baking sheet. Broil 3 to 4 minutes on each side until leaves are lightly charred. Transfer to serving plates. Carefully remove wooden picks and serve at once with a crisp green salad.

Makes 4 servings.

Note: Use a lowfat cream cheese instead of the goat cheese, if preferred.

SPINACH PATTIES

1 pound spinach leaves, rinsed
1/4 cup (2 oz.) cream cheese
1 tablespoon freshly grated Parmesan cheese
2 eggs
1 cup fresh white bread crumbs
Vegetable oil, for frying
WALNUT SAUCE:
2/3 cup walnuts, toasted
1/4 cup fresh white bread crumbs
1 tablespoon walnut oil
1/3 cup milk
1 teaspoon lemon juice
1 teaspoon chopped fresh tarragon
Salt and pepper
Tarragon sprigs, to garnish

In a large saucepan, cook spinach with only the water that clings to leaves 2 to 3 minutes or until just wilted. Cool slightly, then drain and squeeze out excess liquid. Set aside to cool completely. Meanwhile, prepare sauce: In a food processor or blender, process walnuts until finely ground. Add bread crumbs and oil and, with motor running, gradually add milk through the food tube, processing until smooth. Stir in remaining sauce ingredients and season to taste.

Finely chop cooled spinach. Beat in cream cheese and Parmesan cheese, 1 egg, salt and pepper until mixed. In a small bowl, beat remaining egg. Form spinach mixture into 8 patties. Dip first into beaten egg, then into bread crumbs until well coated. In a small skillet, heat oil. Add patties; cook 3 to 4 minutes on each side until golden-brown. Drain well on paper towels. Serve hot, warm or cold with walnut sauce. Garnish with tarragon.

Makes 4 servings.

—POTATO & TOMATO GALETTE—

3 potatoes, scrubbed
2 tablespoons butter or margarine, melted
4 ripe plum tomatoes
6 large basil leaves, shredded
Salt and pepper
2 tablespoons olive oil
Basil or parsley sprigs, to garnish

Preheat oven to 450F (230C). Lightly grease a 9-inch pizza pan or shallow cake pan. Slice potatoes very thinly. Arrange half the potatoes in concentric circles over bottom of pan.

Brush with butter and top with remaining potato slices. Brush again with butter. Cover loosely with foil. Bake 30 minutes. Remove foil and bake 15 minutes longer until golden-brown.

Preheat oil. With a sharp knife, slice tomatoes thinly. Arrange over potatoes. Sprinkle basil over tomatoes, season with salt and pepper and drizzle with oil. Broil 3 to 4 minutes or until bubbling. Cut into quarters and serve hot, garnished with basil or parsley.

Makes 4 servings.

──CORN & PEPPER FRITTERS──

2/3 cup coarse cornmeal
1/2 cup all-purpose flour
1/2 teaspoon each salt and sugar
1 egg, separated
1/2 cup milk
1 tablespoon hazelnut oil or olive oil
2/3 cup plain yogurt
1 teaspoon lemon juice
2 teaspoons chopped fresh mint
1/4 teaspoon ground cumin
1 tablespoon chopped fresh cilantro
3/4 cup cooked whole-kernel corn
1/2 cup diced red bell pepper
1 teaspoon chopped green chile
Vegetable oil, for frying
Mint sprigs, to garnish

In a bowl, combine cornmeal, flour, salt and sugar. Make a well in center and beat in egg yolk, milk and oil until smooth. Cover and refrigerate 1 hour. In a bowl, blend yogurt, lemon juice, mint, cumin and salt. Cover and refrigerate until required. Remove batter from refrigerator and stir in cilantro, corn, bell pepper and chile. Stiffly beat egg white and fold in until evenly incorporated.

In a small heavy skillet, heat about 1/2 inch oil until a drop of water sizzles on contact. Drop in tablespoons of the corn mixture in batches of 3 to 4 and fry 1 to 2 minutes on each side until golden. Drain well on paper towels and keep warm while frying remaining fritters. Serve hot with yogurt sauce and mint sprigs.

Makes 16 fritters.

— VEGETABLES WITH TWO OILS —

1/2 cup virgin olive oil
2 garlic cloves, peeled
1/2 teaspoon coriander seeds, bruised
1/2 teaspoon fennel seeds, bruised
2 lemon peel strips
2 thyme sprigs, bruised
1/3 cup peanut oil
1/2 teaspoon sesame oil
2 gingerroot slices, bruised
1 small shallot, sliced
1 teaspoon soy sauce
1/2 teaspoon crushed dried red chiles
1/2 teaspoon Sechuan peppers, bruised
1-1/2 pounds mixed baby vegetables

In a pan, heat 1 tablespoon of the olive oil.
Add garlic cloves, cilantro seeds and fennel
seeds; cook 5 minutes or until golden. Cool
and transfer to a jar with a lid. Add remaining
olive oil, lemon peel and thyme. Seal jar and
set aside. In a second jar, mix together peanut
oil, sesame oil and all remaining ingredients,
except the vegetables. Leave both oils to
infuse 1 to 2 days.

When ready to serve, transfer the 2 oils to
small bowls. Rinse and trim vegetables as
necessary and serve as crudités with oils and
slices of fresh Italian bread.

Makes 6 servings.

Note: Choose from a selection of your
favorite vegetables, such as radishes, asparagus, broccoli, cauliflower, carrots, bell
peppers, celery and fennel. Lightly cooked
vegetables can also be used as crudités.

BAKED MUSHROOMS

1/3 cup shredded coconut
6 large open cap mushrooms
1/3 cup butter or margarine, softened, or olive oil
1 garlic clove, crushed
Grated peel and juice of 1 lime
1/2 teaspoon grated gingerroot
1 tablespoon chopped fresh cilantro
Salt and pepper
Lemon slices and cilantro leaves, to garnish

Preheat oven to 400F (205C). On a baking sheet, place coconut. Bake 2 to 3 minutes or until browned. Remove from oven and cool slightly.

Trim mushrooms, discarding stems. In a large roasting pan, place mushrooms trimmed-side up. Cream butter, coconut and remaining ingredients together. Spread over inside of mushrooms. Cover loosely with foil. Bake 15 to 20 minutes or until mushrooms are tender. Serve hot with fresh bread to soak up the juices. Garnish with lemon slices and cilantro leaves.

Makes 4 servings.

VEGETABLE FRITTERS

2 tablespoons olive oil
1/2 yellow bell pepper, diced
1-1/4 cups cherry tomatoes, halved
2 tablespoons red-wine vinegar
1-1/2 tablespoons sugar
3 cardamom pods, bruised
1-1/4 cups all-purpose flour
1 tablespoon chopped fresh cilantro
Salt
1 small eggplant
2 small zucchini
1 red bell pepper
4 ounces baby corn-on-the-cobs, trimmed
12 button mushrooms
Vegetable oil, for deep-frying
1 egg white

In a pan, heat 1 tablespoon of the olive oil. Add diced bell pepper; cook 2 minutes, then add tomatoes and stir-fry 1 minute. Add 1-1/2 tablespoons of the vinegar, the sugar, cardamom and 2 tablespoons water. Boil rapidly 5 minutes. Let cool. In a bowl, mix the flour, cilantro and 1 teaspoon salt. Beat in 1 cup iced water and remaining oil and vinegar to form a thick batter. Let stand 30 minutes. Cut the eggplant into thin slices, the zucchini into 1/2-inch slices and the bell pepper into thick strips.

Blanch the baby corn 2 minutes, refresh under cold water and pat dry. Wipe mushrooms. Heat vegetable oil to 350F (175C). Stiffly beat egg white and fold into batter. Dip vegetables into batter, a few at a time, and shake off excess. Fry 2 minutes until crisp and golden. Place vegetable fritters in a warm oven and continue frying remaining fritters. Serve hot with tomato relish.

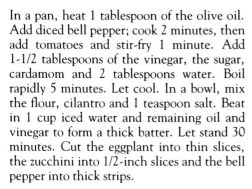

Makes 6 servings.

— ARTICHOKES & MAYONNAISE —

6 large artichokes
1 lemon, halved
1 cup low-calorie mayonnaise
Grated peel 1 of lemon
Juice of 1/2 lemon
2 tablespoons chopped fresh dill
Salt and pepper
Lemon peel strips and fresh dill sprigs, to garnish

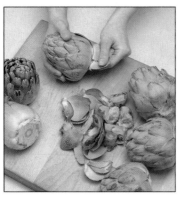

Snap off the long stems from artichokes and cut away tough outer leaves. Trim and discard top 2 inches. Into a large pan of boiling water, drop artichokes. Add halved lemon, cover and cook 30 minutes until leaves easily pull away. Drain artichokes and place into cold water. Leave until cool enough to handle.

In a small bowl, blend together mayonnaise, grated lemon peel, lemon juice and dill. Season to taste with salt and pepper. Scoop out choke from each artichoke. Trim away any tough leaves that remain; cut artichokes in half. Serve cold with the mayonnaise, garnished with lemon peel and dill.

Makes 6 servings.

—FENNEL WITH FETA & PEARS—

2 fennel bulbs
4 tablespoons olive oil
6 ounces vegetarian feta cheese
1 ripe pear
4 sun-dried tomatoes in oil, drained and sliced
1/4 cup pitted ripe olives
Few basil leaves
1 teaspoon lemon juice
1/2 teaspoon honey
Salt and pepper

Preheat broiler. Trim fennel, discarding any damaged outer leaves. Cut each bulb, lengthwise, into 6 thin slices.

Brush each fennel piece with a little olive oil. Place on a baking sheet. Broil 2 to 3 minutes or until browned. Turn fennel, brush with oil and broil 2 to 3 minutes until charred and just tender. Cool slightly.

With a sharp knife, slice feta cheese into thin slabs. Quarter, core and thinly slice pear. Arrange fennel, cheese and pear on serving plates. Top with the tomatoes, olives and basil. In a small bowl, blend remaining oil, lemon juice, honey, salt and pepper together. Drizzle over salad and serve.

Makes 4 servings.

—CARROT & GINGER SOUFFLÉS—

1/2 cup blanched almonds, finely ground and toasted
2 cups chopped carrots
1 tablespoon olive oil
1 small onion, finely chopped
2 teaspoons grated gingerroot
3 tablespoons butter or margarine
3 tablespoons all-purpose flour
1 cup milk
2 cups shredded vegetarian Cheddar cheese
1/2 cup shredded vegetarian Cheshire cheese
3 eggs, separated

Preheat oven to 375F (190C); lightly oil 8 (1-cup) ramekins.

Sprinkle inside of each ramekin with ground almonds to coat sides. Shake out excess and reserve. In a pan of boiling water, cook carrots 15 minutes or until soft. In a small pan, heat oil. Add onion and gingerroot; cook 10 minutes or until softened. Drain carrots. In a blender or food processor, puree carrots and onion mixture until smooth.

In a small pan, melt butter. Stir in flour and cook 1 minute. Gradually add milk; cook, stirring, until thickened. Remove from heat. Stir in cheese. Cool and beat in egg yolks, carrot puree and remaining almonds. Stiffly beat egg whites and fold into cheese mixture. Spoon into prepared ramekins. Place in a roasting pan and add enough boiling water to come two-thirds the way up sides of dishes. Bake 30 minutes or until browned, then serve at once.

Makes 8 servings.

WHITE BEAN PÂTÉ

1/2 cup dried navy beans, soaked overnight in cold
    water to cover
1 bay leaf
2 green onions, chopped
1 small garlic clove, chopped
2 teaspoons chopped fresh cilantro
1/4 teaspoon ground cumin
Pinch of red (cayenne) pepper
1 teaspoon lemon juice
1 tablespoon olive oil
Salt
Ripe olives slices, cilantro sprigs and olive oil, to
    garnish
Pita bread, toasted, and raw vegetables, to serve

Drain soaked beans. In a saucepan, place
beans and cover with cold water. Add bay
leaf and boil rapidly 10 minutes. Reduce
heat, cover and simmer 45 to 50 minutes or
until beans are tender. Drain, reserving 1
tablespoon of the liquid. Discard bay leaf. Let
cool.

Into a blender or food processor, place beans
and reserved liquid. Add onions, garlic,
cilantro, cumin, cayenne, lemon juice, olive
oil and salt; puree to form a smooth paste.
Transfer to a bowl and garnish with olive
slices and cilantro and drizzle with a little oil.
Serve with pita bread and vegetables.

Makes 6 to 8 servings.

—CHICKPEA & PEPPER OMELET—

2 tablespoons olive oil
1 red onion, chopped
1 red bell pepper, chopped
2 garlic cloves, crushed
1 cup cooked chickpeas
1 teaspoon ground turmeric
2 tablespoons chopped fresh parsley
4 large eggs
Salt and pepper
Parsley sprigs and tomato wedges, to garnish

In a nonstick skillet, heat oil. Add onion, bell pepper and garlic; cook 10 minutes or until light golden and softened. Add chickpeas, mashing them lightly. Stir in turmeric and parsley. Stir-fry 2 minutes. Lightly beat eggs with salt and pepper and stir into pan until evenly mixed.

Cook over medium heat 5 to 6 minutes or until cooked and browned underneath. Loosen around edges with a spatula. Carefully slip omelet out onto a plate. Invert pan over omelet and flip over so top is now on bottom. Cook 3 to 4 minutes longer or until golden on bottom. Turn out onto a plate. Cool to room temperature. Garnish with parsley and tomato wedges.

Makes 6 servings.

HAZELNUT CREPES WITH SPINACH

2/3 cup all-purpose flour
1 tablespoon hazelnuts, toasted and finely ground
Salt and pepper
1 egg, lightly beaten
1-1/4 cups milk
1 tablespoon butter or margarine, melted
6 ounces fresh spinach, rinsed
3/4 cup (6 oz.) lowfat cream cheese
1 small garlic clove, crushed
1 tablespoon chopped fresh mixed herbs
2 tablespoons olive oil
1 teaspoon lemon juice
1/4 teaspoon freshly grated nutmeg
Pinch of ground dried chiles

In a bowl, combine flour, hazelnuts and 1/2 teaspoon salt. Gradually beat in egg, milk and butter to form a thin batter; set aside 30 minutes. In a large pan, cook spinach with only the water that clings to leaves 1 minute or until just wilted. Drain well and squeeze out excess water. Chop finely and cool. Beat spinach with cheese, garlic, herbs, 1 tablespoon of the oil, lemon juice, spices, salt and pepper to form a paste.

Brush an omelet pan or small skillet with a little of the remaining oil. Place over medium heat. When hot, pour in a little batter, swirl mixture over bottom of pan and cook 1 to 2 minutes until browned on bottom. Turn over and cook other side 30 seconds or until golden. Transfer to a plate and keep warm. Repeat to make 12 crepes. Spread each with a little spinach and cheese mixture, then fold into quarters. Serve at once.

Makes 4 to 6 servings.

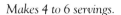

VEGETABLE GRATIN

2/3 cup long-grain rice
3 zucchini
1 red bell pepper
1 onion
6 ripe tomatoes
2 tablespoons olive oil
2 fresh thyme sprigs, chopped
2 fresh rosemary sprigs, chopped
2 bay leaves
1 teaspoon dried leaf oregano
1 teaspoon fennel seeds, toasted
2/3 cup vegetable stock (page 65)
3/4 cup shredded vegetarian Cheddar cheese

Preheat oven to 400F (205C). Into a small pan, put rice. Cover with cold water. Bring to a boil and cook 3 minutes. Drain well and transfer to a casserole dish. Cut zucchini into thick slices, cut bell pepper and onion into 1/2-inch pieces and chop tomatoes.

Into a large bowl, place prepared vegetables. Add oil and stir to coat vegetables with oil. Add thyme, rosemary, bay leaves, oregano and fennel seeds. Stir and spoon over rice. Pour stock over vegetables, cover with foil and bake 40 minutes. Remove foil, sprinkle with cheese and bake 10 to 15 minutes or until cheese is melted and all liquid is absorbed. Brown under a hot broiler, if desired, and serve hot.

Makes 6 servings.

── MUSHROOM & BEAN CHILI ──

4 tablespoons olive oil
1 large eggplant, diced
6 ounces button mushrooms, wiped
1 large onion, chopped
1 garlic clove, chopped
1-1/2 teaspoons paprika
1 teaspoon chili powder
1 teaspoon ground coriander
1/2 teaspoon ground cumin
2 pounds tomatoes, peeled and chopped
2/3 cup vegetable stock (page 65)
10 tortilla chips
1 tablespoon tomato paste
1 (14-oz.) can red kidney beans
1 tablespoon chopped fresh cilantro
Salt and pepper

In a large pan, heat 2 tablespoons of the oil. Add eggplant; stir-fry 10 minutes or until browned. Remove from pan with a slotted spoon. Add 1 tablespoon of the oil to the pan, add mushrooms and stir-fry until browned. Remove with a slotted spoon. Add remaining oil to pan. Add onion, garlic and spices; cook 5 minutes. Add tomatoes and stock and cook, covered, 45 minutes.

Finely crush tortilla chips. Blend with 4 tablespoons water and tomato paste. Beat into chili sauce and add mushrooms and eggplant. Drain beans and add to pan with cilantro. Cover and cook 20 minutes longer. Season and serve with cooked rice and sour cream, if desired.

Makes 6 servings.

Note: Check the package label to ensure that the tortilla chips are cooked in vegetable oil.

PARSNIP, PEAR & ALMOND SAUTÉ

12 pearl onions
3 tablespoons olive oil
1-1/4 pounds baby parsnips, halved or quartered
1 garlic clove, chopped
2 teaspoons chopped fresh thyme
1/2 cup cider
2/3 cup vegetable stock (page 65)
1 tablespoon brown sugar
2 teaspoons whole-grain mustard
2 small pears, cored and thickly sliced
1/2 cup blanched almonds, toasted
Salt and pepper

In a small pan, place onions. Cover with cold water and bring to a boil. Drain and refresh under cold water. Peel parsnips and cut in half. In a large skillet, heat 2 tablespoons of the oil. Add onions, parsnips, garlic and thyme; stir-fry 10 minutes or until browned. Add cider and boil rapidly 5 minutes. In a small bowl, blend stock, sugar and mustard together. Stir into pan. Cover and cook 10 to 12 minutes or until parsnips are tender.

Meanwhile, heat remaining oil in another skillet. Add pears; cook over high heat 1 minute on each side or until browned, then remove pears with a slotted spoon. Pour juices from parsnips into skillet. Boil rapidly 2 to 3 minutes or until thickened. Pour over parsnips, add pears and almonds. Heat through. Season with salt and pepper and serve at once.

Makes 4 servings.

BROCCOLI CAPONATA

2 tablespoons olive oil
1 red onion, chopped
1 red bell pepper, chopped
1 garlic clove, chopped
1 teaspoon chopped fresh thyme
1/3 cup dry red wine
1 pound tomatoes, peeled and chopped
2/3 cup vegetable stock (page 65)
1 tablespoon red-wine vinegar
1 tablespoon brown sugar
2-2/3 cups chopped broccoli
2 tablespoons tomato paste
1/2 cup pitted green olives
1/4 cup capers, drained
1 tablespoon shredded fresh basil

In a large pan, heat oil. Add onion, bell pepper, garlic and thyme; cook 6 to 8 minutes or until lightly browned. Add wine and boil rapidly 3 minutes. Add tomatoes, stock, vinegar and sugar. Stir well, then cover and simmer 20 minutes.

Steam broccoli over boiling water 5 minutes or until crisp-tender. Add tomato mixture, tomato paste, olives, capers and basil. Cook 3 to 4 minutes. Cool to room temperature and serve.

Makes 4 servings.

— VEGETABLE & FRUIT CURRY —

1-1/2 teaspoons each coriander seeds and cumin seeds
4 tablespoons vegetable oil
1 large onion, chopped
2 carrots, chopped
2 potatoes, diced
3 garlic cloves, crushed, or 1 tablespoon garlic paste
2 teaspoons grated gingerroot
1 teaspoon each curry powder and turmeric
1 pound tomatoes, peeled and chopped
2 cups vegetable stock (page 65)
1 cup frozen green peas, thawed
1 apple, chopped
1 mango, chopped
2/3 cup cashews, toasted
1 ounce creamed coconut
1 tablespoon chopped fresh cilantro

In a small pan, roast coriander seeds and cumin seeds until browned. In a blender or spice grinder, grind seeds. In a large pan, heat 2 tablespoons of the oil. Add onion, carrots and potatoes; cook 10 minutes or until browned. In a medium-size pan, heat remaining oil. Add garlic, gingerroot, ground spices, curry powder and turmeric; cook 5 minutes. Add tomatoes. Cover and cook 10 minutes. Stir tomato mixture and stock into carrot mixture; simmer 20 minutes.

Add peas, apple and mango. Cook 5 minutes longer. Grind half the cashews and mix with creamed coconut in a small bowl. Stir in enough pan juices to form a paste. Carefully stir into curry until evenly combined. Heat through and serve at once, sprinkled with the whole cashews and cilantro.

Makes 4 to 6 servings.

TOMATO & BEAN TIAN

3 tablespoons olive oil
1 red onion, chopped
1 garlic clove, crushed
1 large red bell pepper, chopped
1 tablespoon chopped fresh thyme
2 teaspoons chopped fresh rosemary
1 (14-oz.) can chopped tomatoes
1 (15-oz.) can cannellino beans, drained
1/2 cup each fresh bread crumbs, chopped pine nuts
    and grated Parmesan cheese or shredded vegetarian
    Cheddar cheese
2 large zucchini, thinly sliced
2 beefsteak tomatoes, thinly sliced
Rosemary sprigs, to garnish

Preheat oven to 375F (190C). In a saucepan, heat 2 tablespoons of the oil. Add onion, garlic, bell pepper, 2 teaspoons of the thyme and 1 teaspoon of the rosemary; cook 5 minutes. Add tomatoes. Cover and cook 20 minutes. Stir in beans and transfer to a shallow baking dish.

In a small bowl, mix bread crumbs, pine nuts and cheese together. Sprinkle half of the mixture over tomato layer. Arrange zucchini and beefsteak tomatoes in rows over the top. Sprinkle with remaining crumb mixture. Drizzle a little remaining oil and herbs over top, if desired. Cover with foil. Bake 30 minutes. Remove foil and bake 15 to 20 minutes or until golden. Garnish with rosemary sprigs and serve hot.

Makes 4 to 6 servings.

BUTTERNUT SQUASH CRUMBLE

1-1/2 pounds butternut squash (about 3 small squash)
1 small fennel bulb, trimmed
1 garlic clove, crushed
1 tablespoon chopped fresh sage
1 (14-oz.) can chopped tomatoes
2/3 cup whipping cream
Salt and pepper
1 cup whole-wheat flour
1/4 cup butter or margarine, diced
1/3 cup macadamia nuts, chopped
1/4 cup grated Parmesan cheese or vegetarian Cheddar
   cheese

Preheat oven to 400F (205C). Peel squash, cut in half and scrape out and discard squash seeds. Cut flesh into 1/2-inch pieces. In a large baking dish, place squash pieces. Cut fennel crosswise into very thin slices. Scatter over squash with garlic and sage. Pour in tomatoes and cream and add a little salt and pepper.

In a bowl, put flour. Cut in butter until the mixture resembles fine bread crumbs. Stir in nuts and cheese. Sprinkle topping over squash. Cover with foil. Bake 40 minutes. Remove foil and bake 15 to 20 minutes longer or until topping is golden and squash is tender.

Makes 6 servings.

CHEESE & EGG STRATA

2-1/2 cups milk
1 bay leaf
2 cardamom pods, bruised
1 tablespoon butter
1 onion, thinly sliced
1/2 teaspoon chopped fresh thyme
1/2 cup sun-dried tomatoes in oil, drained and chopped
1/4 cup Mascarpone cheese
2 cups shredded vegetarian Cheddar cheese
12 whole-wheat bread slices
3 eggs
Pinch of grated nutmeg
Salt and pepper

Preheat oven to 400F (205C). Lightly oil a 9-cup deep, oval baking dish. Into a small pan, put milk, bay leaf and cardamom pods. Heat until almost boiling. Remove from heat and leave to infuse 10 minutes. Strain into a bowl. In a skillet, melt butter. Add onion and thyme; cook 10 minutes or until softened. Add tomatoes. Remove from heat, cool slightly and stir in Mascarpone cheese and 1/2 cup Cheddar cheese.

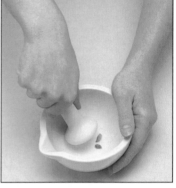

Spread half of onion mixture over bottom of dish. Top with half of the bread and remaining onion mixture. Sprinkle with half of the remaining cheese. Top with remaining bread. Beat eggs, nutmeg, salt and pepper into milk. Pour into baking dish. Sprinkle remaining cheese over top. Place dish in a roasting pan. Pour in boiling water to come two-thirds of the way up side of dish. Cover with foil and bake 30 minutes. Remove foil and bake 20 minutes longer.

Makes 6 to 8 servings.

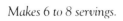

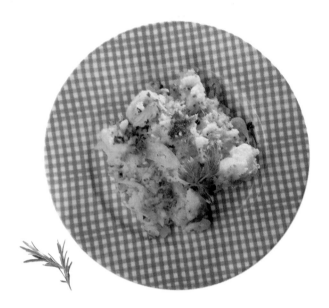

– VEGETARIAN HASH POTATOES –

1-1/4 pounds potatoes, peeled
3 tablespoons butter or margarine
1 onion, thinly sliced
1 teaspoon chopped fresh sage
1 teaspoon chopped fresh rosemary
1/3 cup plain yogurt
1/3 cup shredded vegetarian Cheddar cheese
1 teaspoon whole-grain mustard
1 teaspoon Worcestershire sauce

Cut potatoes into chunks. In a pan, place potatoes. Cover with cold water and bring to a boil. Cook 15 to 20 minutes or until tender. Drain and mash into small pieces.

In a large, nonstick skillet, melt 1 tablespoon of the butter. Add onion and herbs; cook 10 minutes or until onion is soft and golden. In a small bowl, combine remaining ingredients.

Add mashed potatoes to skillet. Stir in yogurt mixture, flattening mixture out to sides of pan. Cook over high heat 5 to 6 minutes or until golden on bottom. Using a spatula, turn potatoes, a little at a time, and brown other side. Serve from pan.

Makes 4 servings.

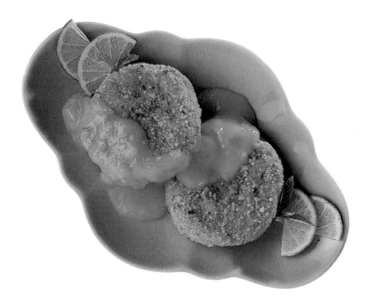

POTATO CAKES & MANGO SAUCE

1/2 pound potatoes, peeled
1 (4-oz.) butternut squash, peeled
1 tablespoon butter or margarine, diced
1 egg yolk
1/3 cup shredded Cheddar cheese
1 tablespoon grated onion
2 teaspoons chopped fresh cilantro
All-purpose flour seasoned with salt and pepper
1 egg, beaten
3/4 cup Brazil nuts, ground
1 small mango, chopped
1 green onion, chopped
1 small garlic clove, crushed
1/2 small fresh green chile, seeded and chopped
Juice of 1 lime
Vegetable oil, for deep-frying

Cube potatoes and squash. In a pan of boiling water, cook until tender. Drain and mash well. Stir in butter, egg yolk and cheese until melted. Stir in onion and cilantro and season to taste. Leave until cold. Shape mixture into 8 small patties. Dust with seasoned flour, then dip into egg and then into ground nuts to coat on all sides.

In a blender or food processor, place all remaining ingredients except oil. Puree until fairly smooth; stir in a little water if the sauce is too thick. In a nonstick skillet, heat 1/2 inch vegetable oil. Add potato cakes, in batches; fry 2 to 3 minutes on each side until golden. Drain well on paper towels. Serve hot with the mango sauce.

Makes 8 servings.

— BRAISED FENNEL PROVENÇAL —

3 fennel bulbs
3 tablespoons olive oil
4 garlic cloves, peeled
1 pound plum tomatoes, peeled and diced
2/3 cup dry white wine
12 Niçoise olives
4 fresh thyme sprigs
2 bay leaves
Pinch of sugar
Salt and pepper
Thyme sprigs, to garnish

Cut fennel bulbs lengthwise into 1/2-inch slices.

In a large skillet, heat oil. Add fennel slices and garlic; cook 4 to 5 minutes on each side or until golden. Remove from pan with a slotted spoon and set aside.

Add tomatoes and wine to pan and boil rapidly 5 minutes. Stir in olives, herbs and sugar. Arrange fennel slices over tomatoes, in a single layer, if possible. Cover and simmer 20 minutes. Season with salt and pepper and serve hot or at room temperature, garnished with thyme.

Makes 4 servings.

BAKED EGGS WITH MOZZARELLA

1 large ripe tomato
1 green onion, chopped
1/3 cup shredded mozzarella cheese
4 pitted ripe olives, sliced
1 tablespoon shredded fresh basil
Salt and pepper
1/3 cup whipping cream
4 eggs
Parsley sprigs, to garnish
Bread slices, toasted, or Melba toast, to serve

Preheat oven to 375F (190C); lightly butter 4 ramekins. Peel and seed tomato and finely dice flesh.

In a small bowl, combine tomato, green onion, cheese, olives, basil, salt and pepper. Divide among ramekins.

In a small pan, heat cream until almost boiling. Pour over tomato mixture and break an egg into each dish. Place in a roasting pan and pour in enough boiling water to come two-thirds up sides of ramekins. Bake 10 to 15 minutes until eggs are just set. Cool slightly, garnish with parsley and serve with toasted bread or Melba toast.

Makes 4 servings.

EGG & SPINACH CUPS

1/2 pound spinach
2 tablespoons butter or margarine, diced
1 cup vegetarian blue cheese, crumbled
1/2 cup whipping cream
Pinch of grated nutmeg
Salt and pepper
4 eggs
4 dill sprigs, to garnish
French bread slices, to serve

Preheat oven to 375F (190C); lightly butter 4 ramekins. Rinse spinach and discard any thick stems.

In a large pan, cook spinach with only the water that clings to leaves 1 to 2 minutes or until just wilted. Drain, squeeze out excess liquid and chop finely. Transfer to a bowl. Beat in butter and cheese until melted, then stir in 1/3 cup of the cream, the nutmeg, salt and pepper.

Divide mixture among ramekins. Make a small hollow in center of each one. Break an egg into each hollow and spoon remaining cream over eggs. Place in a roasting pan. Pour in enough boiling water to come two-thirds up sides of ramekins. Bake 20 to 30 minutes or until eggs feel firm to the touch. Serve hot with French bread and garnish with dill sprigs.

Makes 4 servings.

FRESH HERB FRITTATA

6 eggs
2 egg whites
2 green onions, chopped
1/2 cup cottage cheese
1/2 cup fresh chopped mixed herbs
1 cup arugula leaves
Salt and pepper
1/4 cup olive oil

In a bowl, beat eggs and egg whites together until thoroughly mixed. Stir in green onions, cheese and herbs. Roughly chop arugula leaves and add to mixture with salt and pepper.

Preheat broiler. In a nonstick skillet, heat oil. Pour in egg mixture, swirling to reach edges of pan. Cook, stirring, over medium-low heat about 3 minutes or until eggs are beginning to set.

Place pan under hot broiler 2 to 3 minutes or until set and lightly browned. Turn out onto a plate. Cut into wedges and serve warm or cold with a tomato and olive salad.

Makes 2 or 3 servings.

CORN BREAD MUFFINS

1-1/3 cups cornmeal
1 cup all-purpose flour
2 tablespoons sugar
2 teaspoons baking powder
1 cup buttermilk
1/4 cup butter or margarine, melted
1 egg, lightly beaten
1/4 cup maple syrup
Fresh figs, maple syrup and whipped cream, to serve

Preheat the oven to 400F (205C); lightly oil a 12-cup muffin pan. Into a large bowl, stir cornmeal, flour, sugar and baking powder.

Gradually beat buttermilk, butter, egg and maple syrup until just combined. Do not overmix.

Spoon into prepared muffin pan. Bake 20 minutes or until muffins spring back when pressed in centers. Cool slightly and turn out onto a wire rack to cool completely. Slice figs into wedges and serve with the muffins, a little extra maple syrup and spoonfuls of whipped cream.

Makes 12 muffins.

——ITALIAN BREAD PIZZA——

4 thick slices Italian bread, cut from a large loaf
2 garlic cloves, halved
4 teaspoons sun-dried tomato paste
8 small plum tomatoes, thinly sliced
12 to 16 basil leaves, shredded
5 ounces mozzarella cheese, thinly sliced
1 tablespoon capers in brine, drained
12 pitted green olives, halved
Olive oil

Preheat oven to 475F (240C). Cut each bread slice in half crosswise.

Under a hot broiler, toast bread lightly on both sides. Rub with garlic. Spread one side of each piece with tomato paste.

Arrange tomatoes over tomato paste; sprinkle with basil leaves. Top with cheese, capers and olives. Drizzle with a little oil. Bake 8 to 10 minutes or until cheese melts Serve hot.

Makes 4 servings.

BLUE CHEESE PIZZAS

1/2 cup pitted ripe olives
1 garlic clove, chopped
1 teaspoon chopped fresh thyme
1 tablespoon olive oil
1 recipe Pizza Dough (opposite page)
3 tablespoons butter
2 red onions, thinly sliced
1/2 teaspoon fennel seeds
1 teaspoon chopped fresh rosemary
3 ounces vegetarian blue cheese, crumbled
Grated peel of 1 lemon
Rosemary sprigs, to garnish

In a blender or food processor, puree olives, garlic, thyme and oil to form a smooth paste.

Make Pizza Dough. Cover and let rise in a warm place 30 minutes. In a skillet, melt butter. Add onions; cook over low heat 20 to 25 minutes or until golden. Let cool. Preheat oven to 450F (230C); place a baking sheet or pizza stone on top shelf.

Divide pizza dough into 4 pieces. Roll out each piece on a lightly floured surface to a 5-inch circle. Spread olive paste and onion mixture over each circle. Sprinkle with fennel seeds and rosemary, then cheese. Sprinkle with lemon peel and transfer pizzas to hot baking sheet. Bake 10 to 12 minutes or until bubbly and golden. Serve hot, garnished with rosemary.

Makes 4 servings.

— BROILED VEGETABLE PIZZA —

1 red bell pepper, quartered
1 small zucchini, sliced
1 small eggplant, sliced
1 small onion, thinly sliced
6 large tomatoes, quartered and seeded
2 tablespoons prepared pesto sauce
Salt and pepper
1-1/4 cups shredded vegetarian mozzarella cheese
PIZZA DOUGH:
1-2/3 cups all-purpose flour
1/2 teaspoon quick-rise dried yeast
1/2 teaspoon salt
1/2 cup warm water
1 tablespoon olive oil

To prepare dough: In a bowl, mix flour, yeast and salt together. Make a well in center; stir in water and oil to form a stiff dough. Knead 5 minutes. Place in a greased bowl, cover and let rise in a warm place 30 minutes or until doubled in size. Preheat oven to 450F (230C) and place a baking sheet or pizza stone on top shelf. Place pepper, zucchini, eggplant and onion on a rack in a baking sheet; brush with a little oil. Broil until charred on all sides.

Broil tomato quarters, skin-sides up, until blistered. Peel and discard skin and mash flesh with pesto sauce, salt and pepper. Roll out dough to a 9-inch circle. Spread tomato mixture over dough; arrange broiled vegetables over top. Sprinkle with cheese. Transfer to hot baking sheet or pizza stone. Bake 25 to 30 minutes until bubbly and golden.

Makes 4 servings.

- PENNE WITH LEEKS & RICOTTA -

1 pound leeks, rinsed
2 to 3 tablespoons hazelnut oil
1 garlic clove, sliced
4 cups dried penne or other pasta shape
Olive oil
1 cup ricotta cheese
1/4 cup milk
1/3 cup freshly grated Pecorino cheese or Parmesan
   cheese
2 tablespoons mixed chopped fresh herbs
1/2 teaspoon grated lemon peel
1/2 teaspoon lemon juice
Salt and pepper
Parsley sprigs, to garnish

Preheat oven to 425F (220C). Cut leeks into thick slices. Into a roasting pan, place leeks with 2 tablespoons of the oil and the garlic. Roast 25 minutes or until lightly browned. After 10 minutes, bring a large pan of water to a boil. Add pasta, a little olive oil and return to a boil. Reduce heat and simmer 10 minutes or until pasta is cooked but still firm to the bite.

Meanwhile, in a small pan, place all remaining ingredients. Stir over low heat until melted. Heat through 5 minutes without boiling. Drain pasta. Stir in a little more hazelnut oil and toss with cooked leeks. Stir in hot cheese mixture, season with salt and pepper and serve at once, garnished with parsley.

Makes 4 servings.

──VEGETARIAN SPAGHETTI──

2 tablespoons hazelnut oil
1 cup fresh bread crumbs
3/4 pound dried spaghetti
1/3 cup virgin olive oil
2 garlic cloves, sliced
Grated peel of 1 lemon
1-1/2 teaspoons chopped fresh rosemary
3 cups thinly sliced zucchini
1/3 cup sliced drained sun-dried tomatoes in oil
2 tablespoons capers, drained
Juice of 1/2 lemon
Salt and pepper

In a large nonstick skillet, heat hazelnut oil. Add bread crumbs; stir-fry over medium heat 3 to 4 minutes or until evenly browned. Remove from heat and set aside. In a pan of boiling water, cook spaghetti with a little olive oil, 8 to 10 minutes or until cooked but still firm to the bite.

In a large skillet, heat 1 teaspoon of the olive oil. Add garlic, lemon peel and rosemary. Cook 30 seconds or until beginning to brown. Add zucchini and stir-fry 3 to 4 minutes or until golden. Add tomatoes and capers; cook 1 minute. Stir in lemon juice, salt and pepper. Drain pasta. Add remaining olive oil and toss until well coated. Serve at once topped with zucchini mixture and the bread crumbs.

Makes 4 servings.

CARAMELIZED CABBAGE & PASTA

1 red bell pepper
1/4 cup butter or margarine
1 large onion, thinly sliced
1 garlic clove, chopped
1 small green cabbage (about 1-1/4 lbs.)
1 tablespoon brown sugar
1 cup dried shell pasta
Salt and black pepper
Chopped fresh parsley, to garnish

Preheat oven to 400F (205C). Under hot broiler, roast bell pepper 20 minutes. Place in a plastic bag and leave until cool enough to handle. Peel, seed and cut flesh into thin strips.

In a large nonstick skillet, melt butter. Add onion and garlic; cook 10 minutes or until lightly browned. Trim outer leaves off cabbage. Cut cabbage into quarters and discard central core. Roughly shred cabbage; stir into onion mixture with sugar. Stir well, cover and cook over very low heat 15 minutes, stirring occasionally, or until cabbage is golden and just tender.

In a pan of lightly salted, boiling water, cook pasta 10 minutes or until tender but still firm to the bite. Drain well. Stir into cabbage with roasted pepper, salt and black pepper. Serve at once, garnished with chopped parsley.

Makes 6 servings.

——TAGLIATELLE WITH BEETS——

1/2 cup butter or margarine, softened
2 tablespoons snipped fresh chives
1 teaspoon grated lemon peel
2 tablespoons walnut oil
1 large onion, thinly sliced
1 teaspoon sugar
2 teaspoons balsamic vinegar
12 ounces beets, cooked and diced
18 ounces fresh tagliatelle
Salt and freshly ground pepper
Small bunch fresh chervil, chopped

In a small bowl, cream butter, chives and lemon peel. Cover and refrigerate 1 hour.

In a nonstick skillet, heat oil over medium heat. Add onion; cook 15 minutes or until evenly golden. Add sugar, vinegar and beets. Stir in three-quarters of the chive butter. Cover and simmer 4 to 5 minutes.

In a pan of boiling water, cook pasta 3 to 4 minutes or until tender but still firm to the bite. Drain well. Season with salt and plenty of pepper. Stir in remaining chive butter to thoroughly coat pasta. Toss with the beet and onion mixture. Serve at once, sprinkled with chervil.

Makes 4 servings.

RADICCHIO RISOTTO

2 tablespoons olive oil
1 large onion, chopped
1 large garlic clove, chopped
1 teaspoon chopped fresh thyme
2 cups risotto rice
1 large head radicchio, shredded
2/3 cup dry red wine
2-1/2 cups vegetable stock (page 65)
2 tablespoons sun-dried tomato paste
Salt and pepper
Chopped fresh parsley, to garnish
Freshly grated Parmesan cheese, to serve

In a large, heavy nonstick skillet, heat oil. Add onion, garlic and thyme; cook 5 minutes or until softened. Add rice. Stir over medium heat 1 minute or until rice is transparent. Stir in radicchio and immediately add wine. Boil rapidly until all liquid has evaporated.

Gradually stir in stock in 3 to 4 batches, cooking over low heat, stirring constantly, 25 minutes or until all stock is absorbed and rice is tender. Stir in tomato paste, salt and pepper. Garnish with chopped parsley. Serve hot with Parmesan cheese.

Makes 6 to 8 servings.

Note: For a vegan recipe, omit cheese.

──LEEK & MUSHROOM PILAF──

1/4 cup dried cep mushrooms
Pinch of saffron strands
2/3 cup boiling water
1-1/4 cups basmati rice
2 cups vegetable stock (page 65)
2 tablespoons olive oil
3 large leeks
4 ounces fresh mushrooms
Salt and pepper
Chives, to garnish

In a small bowl, place ceps and saffron. Add boiling water. Let soak 10 minutes.

Rinse rice under cold running water several minutes until the water runs clear; drain well. In a saucepan, place rice. Add stock and cep mixture. Bring to a boil, stir once, cover and simmer 12 minutes.

Meanwhile, in a skillet, heat oil. Add leeks; cook 3 minutes. Add fresh mushrooms and stir-fry 3 minutes. Keep warm. As soon as rice is tender, stir it into mushroom mixture. Heat through 1 to 2 minutes. Season, garnish with chives and serve at once.

Makes 6 servings.

LEMON VEGETABLE RICE

Juice of 2 lemons
2 tablespoons sugar
About 4 cups vegetable stock (page 65)
1-1/2 cups long-grain rice
1/2 teaspoon salt
1 cinnamon stick
5 whole cloves
2 tablespoons butter or margarine
1 teaspoon cumin seeds
1 small onion, thinly sliced
2 small zucchini
1/3 cup cashews, toasted
2 tablespoons chopped fresh mint
Lime wedges, to garnish

In a 4-cup measure, mix lemon juice and sugar together. Make up to 2-1/2 cups with vegetable stock. Pour mixture into a saucepan. Add rice, salt, cinnamon and cloves. Bring to a boil, stir once and simmer 10 minutes or until all liquid is absorbed. Remove from heat, cover with a tight-fitting lid, let sit undisturbed 10 minutes.

In a small skillet, melt butter. Add cumin seeds; stir-fry 1 to 3 minutes or until they start to pop. Add onion; cook 5 minutes. Cut zucchini into thin slices and add to skillet with cashews and mint. Stir-fry 2 to 3 minutes or until zucchini are tender. Stir in rice. Heat through 1 minute, then serve. Garnish with lime.

Makes 4 to 6 servings.

MUSHROOM & CHEESE SQUARES

2 pounds prepared puff pastry dough
1/4 ounce dried cep mushrooms
2/3 cup boiling water
2 tablespoons olive oil
1 cup diced eggplant
3 cups finely chopped fresh mushrooms
1 garlic clove, crushed
1 teaspoon chopped fresh thyme
2 tablespoons tomato paste
Salt and pepper
1/3 cup diced vegetarian goat cheese
1 egg, beaten
1 tablespoon milk

On a lightly floured surface, roll out dough into 2 (13″ x 9″) rectangles. Cut out 6 (4-inch) squares from each rectangle. Cover and let rest 30 minutes. Into a bowl, place ceps. Add boiling water; let soak 20 minutes. Drain, reserving liquid. Chop and reserve ceps. In a large pan, heat 1 tablespoon of the oil. Add eggplant; stir-fry 3 to 4 minutes. Add ceps, fresh mushrooms, garlic and thyme; stir-fry 3 minutes. Add reserved cep liquid and boil rapidly 3 minutes. Stir in tomato paste, salt and pepper. Let cool.

Preheat oven to 425F (220C). Spread a large spoonful of mushroom mixture in center of 6 dough squares, leaving a narrow border around edges. Top with diced cheese. Dampen edges with a little water and top with remaining squares. Press edges together to seal and cut a small slit in top of each pie. In a small bowl, beat egg and milk together. Brush over each pie. Transfer to a baking sheet. Bake 15 to 18 minutes or until puffed and golden-brown.

Makes 6 servings.

─ VEGETABLE FILO PACKAGES ─

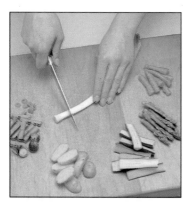

4 small new potatoes, halved
8 baby carrots
8 baby zucchini, halved
8 asparagus tips
1 baby leek, sliced into 8 pieces
1/4 cup butter or margarine, softened
1 tablespoon chopped fresh mint
1/4 teaspoon ground cumin
Pinch red (cayenne) pepper
Salt and pepper
4 large sheets filo pastry
1/3 cup olive oil

Preheat oven to 375F (190C); place a baking sheet on middle shelf.

In a large pan of boiling water, cook potatoes 6 to 8 minutes or until almost cooked. Blanch remaining vegetables 2 to 3 minutes, depending on size, until almost tender. Drain all vegetables. Cool in cold water. Drain and dry thoroughly. Cream together butter, mint, spices, salt and pepper. Take 1 large sheet of dough and, using a 10-inch plate or a pan lid as a template, carefully cut out a circle. Repeat to make 4 circles. Brush liberally with oil.

Place one-quarter of vegetables in a small pile on one side of dough circle. Dot with mint butter. Fold other side of dough over filling, pressing edges together to seal. Brush a little oil along edge and turn over a bit at a time to ensure filling is totally enclosed. Repeat to make 4 packages and transfer to heated cookie sheet. Carefully brush with remaining oil. Bake 12 to 15 minutes or until pastry is golden. Serve immediately.

Makes 4 servings.

─ GOAT CHEESE & FIG TART ─

1-3/4 cups all-purpose flour
Pinch of salt
1/2 cup butter or margarine, chilled
1 egg yolk
2 tablespoons iced water
1 tablespoon olive oil
1 large onion, thinly sliced
2 teaspoons chopped fresh thyme
1/2 teaspoon fennel seeds
4 fresh figs
1/2 cup soft goat cheese
1/4 cup freshly grated Parmesan cheese
2/3 cup dairy sour cream
1 large egg, lightly beaten

Preheat oven to 400F (205C). Into a bowl, sift flour and salt. Cut in butter until mixture resembles fine bread crumbs. Make a well in center and work in egg yolk and water to form a soft dough. On a floured surface, knead. Wrap and refrigerate 30 minutes. Thinly roll out dough and use to line a 9-inch tart pan. Prick bottom and refrigerate 20 minutes. Line with foil and pie weights. Bake blind 10 minutes. Remove foil and weights; bake 10 to 12 minutes or until crisp and golden.

In a skillet, heat oil. Add onion, thyme and fennel; cook 10 minutes. Chop 2 figs, add to pan and remove from heat. Beat goat cheese, Parmesan cheese, sour cream and egg together until smooth. Spread onion mixture into tart shell. Spoon in cheese mixture. Slice remaining figs and arrange around edge of tart. Bake 25 minutes or until set. Serve warm or cold.

Makes 8 servings.

POTATO & ONION TART

3/4 cup all-purpose flour
Pinch of salt
1/2 cup unsalted butter, chilled
1 egg yolk
2 tablespoons iced water
FILLING:
1 pound waxy potatoes
2 tablespoons butter or margarine
2 large onions, thinly sliced
1 teaspoon chopped fresh rosemary
1/2 teaspoon caraway seeds
3/4 cup half and half
1/4 cup shredded vegetarian Cheddar cheese
Freshly grated nutmeg

Preheat oven to 400F (205C). Into a large bowl, sift flour and salt. Cut in butter until mixture resembles fine bread crumbs. Make a well in center. Work in egg yolk and water to form a soft dough. On a lightly floured surface, knead dough. Wrap and refrigerate 30 minutes. Roll out thinly and use to line a deep 9-inch fluted tart pan. Prick bottom. Refrigerate 20 minutes. Line with foil and pie weights. Bake blind 10 minutes. Remove weights and foil and bake 10 to 12 minutes or until crisp.

Increase oven temperature to 450F (230C). Boil potatoes 15 minutes or until just tender. Let cool, carefully peel and cut into very thin slices. Melt butter in a skillet. Add onions, rosemary and caraway seeds; cook 10 minutes or until golden. Spread onion mixture over pastry shell and top with potato slices. Beat remaining ingredients together. Pour over potatoes; bake on top rack 15 minutes or until golden.

Makes 6 to 8 servings.

—OLIVE & MOZZARELLA PUFFS—

1/2 cup pitted green olives
1 ounce mozzarella cheese
2 teaspoons chopped fresh parsley
1/2 teaspoon chopped fresh sage
Pinch of chili powder
1 sheet prepared puff pastry dough from a 17-oz. pkg.,
  thawed if frozen
1 egg
Salt
Parsley leaves and extra olives, to garnish

Preheat oven to 425F (220C); lightly oil a baking sheet. Very finely chop olives and cheese. Mix with herbs and chili powder to form a paste. Set aside.

On a lightly floured surface, roll out pastry dough. Using a 4-inch fluted cookie cutter, cut out 8 circles. Place 1 heaped teaspoon olive mixture in center of each circle. Lightly dampen edges of dough, fold in half to form semicircles, pressing edges together well to seal. Transfer to the baking sheet.

Beat egg with a little salt. Brush over pastries. Cut 2 small slashes in each one. Bake 12 to 15 minutes or until puffed and golden-brown. Serve warm or cold with a salad garnish.

Makes 8 servings.

Note: These make ideal buffet party nibbles. Make up double quantity of filling, cut dough into smaller circles to make bite-sized appetizers.

WINTER VEGETABLE PIE

1-1/4 cups self-rising flour
Salt
8 tablespoons vegetable shortening
2 tablespoons chopped fresh mixed herbs
4 to 5 tablespoons iced water
2 tablespoons olive oil
6 ounces pearl onions, halved
1 garlic clove, chopped
1-1/4 pounds prepared mixed winter vegetables
    (carrots, turnips, parsnips, cauliflower flowerets)
4 ounces button mushrooms
2/3 cup dry red wine
1-1/2 cups vegetable stock (see opposite)
2 tablespoons tomato paste

Into a large bowl, sift flour with 1 teaspoon salt. Cut in 2 tablespoons of the shortening. Stir in half the herbs and work in enough iced water to form a soft dough. Knead lightly. Wrap and refrigerate 30 minutes. Roll out dough to a rectangle about 1/2 inch thick. Dot top two-thirds with 2 tablespoons of the shortening. Bring the bottom third of dough up into middle and top third over this. Press edges to seal. Wrap and refrigerate 30 minutes. Repeat process twice and refrigerate a final 30 minutes.

Preheat oven to 400F (205C). In a skillet, heat oil. Add onions, garlic and vegetables; cook 10 minutes. Add wine and boil 5 minutes. Add stock and tomato paste. Simmer 20 minutes. Transfer to a 5-cup deep oval baking dish.

Roll out dough to a 1/4-inch rectangle. Cut out a pie top a little larger than dish. Cut remaining dough into strips, dampen and press around edge of dish. Dampen edge of dough. Place dough lid over pie and press edges to seal. Bake 30 minutes.

Makes 6 servings.

Note: To make vegetable stock, cook 1 coarsely chopped onion and 1 trimmed and sliced leek in 2 teaspoons olive oil until softened. Add 2 chopped carrots, 1 diced large potato and 2 sliced celery stalks. Cook 5 minutes longer.

Add 4 coarsely chopped ripe tomatoes, 1-1/2 cups quartered mushrooms, 1/3 cup rice, 2 parsley sprigs, 2 thyme sprigs, 1 bay leaf, 1 teaspoon salt, 6 white peppercorns and 5 cups water. Bring to a boil. Cover and simmer 30 minutes. Strain through a fine strainer.

—— BROCCOLI & OLIVE TART ——

Whole-wheat pastry dough for a 9-inch pie
1 yellow bell pepper
1 red bell pepper
4 ounces broccoli flowerets
1/2 cup pitted ripe olives, halved
2 eggs, beaten
1/2 cup half and half
1/2 cup soft goat cheese
2 tablespoons chopped fresh parsley
Salt and pepper

On a lightly floured surface, roll out dough. Use to line a deep 9-inch fluted tart pan. Prick bottom and refrigerate 20 minutes. Preheat oven to 400F (205C). Quarter and seed bell peppers. Broil 4 to 5 minutes or until lightly charred. Let cool slightly, then peel and thinly slice flesh. Steam broccoli 3 minutes.

Line the tart shell with foil and pie weights. Bake blind 10 minutes. Remove weights and foil and bake 10 to 12 minutes longer until pastry is crisp and golden. Cool slightly and arrange bell peppers, broccoli and olives over bottom. Beat remaining ingredients together until smooth. Pour over vegetables. Bake 35 minutes or until set in center. Cool and serve warm or cold.

Makes 6 to 8 servings.

SPINACH RISOTTO CAKE

Pinch of saffron threads
3-1/4 cups hot vegetable stock (page 65)
1/4 cup butter or margarine
1 large onion, finely chopped
1 garlic clove, crushed
1-1/3 cups risotto rice
1/2 pound spinach, trimmed
2 eggs, lightly beaten
1/4 cup mascarpone cheese or dairy sour cream
1/4 cup shredded vegetarian Cheddar cheese
1 tablespoon chopped fresh tarragon
Pinch of grated nutmeg
Salt and pepper

Soak the saffron in hot stock 10 minutes. In a large skillet, melt butter. Add onion and garlic; cook 10 minutes. Add rice. Stir-fry 2 minutes. Add a little stock, simmer until absorbed and continue adding stock gradually until completely absorbed and rice is tender, about 25 minutes. Preheat oven to 400F (205C). Lightly grease an 8-inch springform pan.

In a large pan with only water that clings to leaves, cook spinach until just wilted. Drain well and squeeze out excess liquid. Chop finely. Beat all remaining ingredients together until combined. Stir into cooked rice with spinach. Transfer to prepared pan. Smooth surface and bake 30 minutes or until set.

Makes 8 servings.

Note: Serve with a double recipe of Red Pepper Sauce (page 73).

─── WHOLE CORN BREAD ───

2/3 cup coarse cornmeal
2 cups all-purpose flour
1 teaspoon quick-rise dried yeast
1 teaspoon sugar
1/2 teaspoon salt
1 (8-oz.) can whole-kernel corn kernels
2/3 cup milk
2 tablespoons butter, melted

In a large bowl, combine cornmeal, flour, yeast, sugar and salt. Make a well in center.

Drain corn, reserving juice. Into a small pan, pour juices. Add milk and heat gently until tepid. Stir into cornmeal mixture with melted butter and gradually work to form a soft dough. On a lightly floured surface, knead 6 to 8 minutes or until smooth. Carefully begin working in corn, adding a little more flour, if necessary. In an oiled bowl, place dough, cover and let rise in a warm place 45 minutes or until doubled in size.

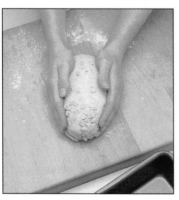

Grease a 9" x 5" loaf pan. Punch down dough, form into a loaf shape and press into loaf pan. Cover and let rise 30 minutes or until dough reaches top of the pan. Preheat oven to 425F (220C). Bake 25 minutes or until browned and bottom sounds hollow when tapped. Let cool on a wire rack before serving.

Makes 1 large loaf.

Note: For vegans, replace butter with 2 tablespoons oil and use soy milk.

—POLENTA WITH MUSHROOMS—

3-3/4 cups vegetable stock (page 65)
1/2 teaspoon salt
1 cup polenta
1 teaspoon chopped fresh thyme
1/2 cup freshly grated Parmesan cheese
2 tablespoons butter
1/2 ounce dried cep mushrooms
1/3 cup boiling water
1/4 cup port wine
3 tablespoons virgin olive oil
1 garlic clove, crushed
1 shallot, finely chopped
5 cups sliced mixed fresh mushrooms, sliced
1 tablespoon chopped fresh parsley

In a large pan, bring 3-1/4 cups of the stock and the salt to a boil. Stir in polenta. Stir, cover and simmer 25 minutes, stirring frequently. Add thyme and cook 5 minutes. Stir in cheese and butter. Spoon polenta mixture into a lightly oiled, shallow pan. Smooth surface and let cool. Soak ceps in the boiling water 20 minutes. Into a pan, strain soaking liquid. Chop ceps. Add port and remaining 1/2 cup stock to pan. Boil rapidly until reduced to about 1/2 cup. Set aside.

Turn out polenta. Cut into 12 triangles. Brush with oil and broil 8 to 10 minutes on each side until golden. Meanwhile, in a large pan, heat oil. Add garlic, shallot and ceps; cook 5 minutes. Add sliced fresh mushrooms and stir-fry 3 to 4 minutes or until browned. Add reduced liquid, cover and cook 5 minutes. Add parsley. Serve broiled polenta triangles with mushroom sauce.

Makes 6 servings.

– PASTA & SQUASH TRIANGLES –

1-1/2 cups all-purpose flour
1 teaspoon salt
6 fresh sage leaves, chopped
2 eggs
1 egg yolk
3 tablespoons olive oil
Shavings of Parmesan cheese, to serve
FILLING:
1-1/3 cups peeled and cubed butternut squash
1 small garlic clove, crushed
1/3 cup ricotta cheese
1/2 cup freshly grated Parmesan cheese
Pinch of grated nutmeg
Salt and pepper

In a large bowl, mix flour, salt and sage. Make a well in center and work in eggs, egg yolk and 1 tablespoon of the oil to form a stiff dough. On a lightly floured surface, knead 5 minutes or until smooth and elastic. Wrap in plastic wrap and let rest 30 minutes.

Prepare filling. Steam squash 10 to 15 minutes until soft. With a fork, mash until smooth. Transfer to a clean pan and heat gently until completely dry. In a bowl, place squash and leave until cold. Beat in garlic, ricotta and Parmesan cheeses, nutmeg and seasoning to taste.

Divide the pasta dough into 4 pieces. Roll out each piece on a lightly floured surface as thinly and evenly as possible. Cut into 3-inch squares.

Place 1 teaspoon squash filling into middle of each square. Dampen the edges and fold in half diagonally to form triangles. Place triangles onto a lightly floured tray to prevent them sticking together.

In a large pan of boiling salted water, add 1 tablespoon of the remaining olive oil. Cook triangles in batches 3 to 5 minutes or until tender. Drain and toss with extra olive oil. Serve with shavings of Parmesan cheese and black pepper.

Makes 4 to 6 servings.

Note: The pasta dough can be made in a food processor. If you have a pasta machine, roll out dough using the thinnest setting.

NOODLES WITH ROASTED TOFU

3/4 pound plain tofu, cubed
2 tablespoons dark soy sauce
1 garlic clove, crushed
1 teaspoon grated peeled gingerroot
1 tablespoon sesame oil
1 tablespoon honey
2 cups vegetable stock (page 65)
1 stem lemon grass, crushed
2 star anise
1 red chile
1 tablespoon olive oil
2 ounces each asparagus spears, oyster mushrooms,
    snow peas, Chinese cabbage, trimmed
1/2 pound fresh pasta noodles
1 tablespoon miso paste

Into a baking dish, place tofu. Mix together soy sauce, garlic, gingerroot, sesame oil and honey. Pour over tofu. Let marinate 2 to 4 hours, stirring from time to time. Preheat oven to 400F (205C). Strain tofu, reserving 1 tablespoon marinade. Transfer tofu to a nonstick baking dish. Roast 30 minutes, turning once, until crisp and golden. Into a pan, put stock, reserved marinade, lemon grass, star anise and chile. Bring to a boil, cover and simmer 25 minutes.

In a large skillet, heat oil. Add asparagus; stir-fry 2 minutes. Add remaining vegetables and stir-fry 1 minute longer. Cook pasta noodles according to package directions. Into skillet, strain stock. Stir in miso paste until combined. Drain pasta. Add to pan and stir in roasted tofu and pan juices. Serve at once.

Makes 4 servings.

Note: For vegans, replace honey with sugar.

—— WATERCRESS CUSTARDS ——

2 red bell peppers
2 tablespoons olive oil
1/2 cup vegetable stock (page 65)
1 tablespoon butter or margarine
4 cups watercress leaves
3 eggs
3/4 cup whipping cream
1/4 cup finely shredded vegetarian Cheddar cheese
1 teaspoon Dijon-style mustard
Salt and pepper

Preheat oven to 400F (205C). Roast peppers 20 to 25 minutes until skins are lightly charred. Transfer to a plastic bag and let cool 30 minutes. Peel peppers, discard seeds, reserving any juices. In a blender or food processor, puree peppers and juices with oil and stock to form a smooth sauce. Press puree through strainer into a small pan. Reduce oven temperature to 350F (175C); grease 6 molds.

In a skillet, melt butter. Add watercress; cook 1 minute or until just wilted. In a blender or food processor, puree watercress. Add eggs, cream, cheese, mustard, salt and pepper; process until smooth. Pour into molds. Place in a roasting pan and pour in enough boiling water to come two-thirds up sides of molds. Bake 25 minutes or until firm in centers. Let rest 5 minutes, then unmold. Serve warm with reheated pepper sauce.

Makes 6 servings.

SPINACH GNOCCHI

3/4 pound trimmed spinach leaves
3/4 cup ricotta cheese
Pinch of freshly grated nutmeg
1/3 cup all-purpose flour
1 large egg, lightly beaten
1/4 cup grated Parmesan cheese or vegetarian Cheddar
  cheese
2 tablespoons olive oil
Salt and pepper
1 (14-oz.) can chopped tomatoes
1 garlic clove, crushed
1 tablespoon chopped fresh basil
Pinch of sugar
4 ounces vegetarian blue cheese
2 tablespoons milk

In a large pan, cook spinach with the water clinging to leaves until wilted. Drain, squeeze out excess liquid and chop finely. Cool and beat in the ricotta cheese, nutmeg, flour, egg, Parmesan cheese, half of the oil, salt and pepper. Refrigerate 2 hours.

In a small pan, put tomatoes, remaining oil, garlic, basil and sugar. Simmer 30 minutes. In a blender or food processor, process mixture until pureed. Keep warm.

Shape ricotta mixture into walnut-size balls to make 32 small gnocchi. Flatten out and place on a floured tray.

Into a large pan of simmering water, drop gnocchi, in batches. Cook 6 minutes. Drain on paper towels and keep warm while cooking remaining gnocchi in same way.

Preheat broiler. In a small pan, gently heat milk and blue cheese, stirring until smooth. Pour tomato sauce over bottom of 4 gratin dishes or flameproof plates. Arrange gnocchi on top and drizzle cheese sauce over top. Broil 3 to 4 minutes until bubbling and golden.

Makes 4 servings.

— ENDIVE ASPARAGUS GRATIN —

20 asparagus spears
4 small heads Belgian endive
1/2 cup virgin olive oil
1 garlic clove, crushed
Grated peel and juice of 1/2 lemon
1 tablespoon chopped fresh basil
1/3 cup freshly grated Parmesan cheese
Salt and pepper

Trim asparagus spears, removing woody ends. Peel almost to tips. Steam spears 2 minutes or until bright green.

Lightly oil 4 small gratin dishes. Preheat broiler. Halve and trim endives. Place 2 halves into each dish. Arrange asparagus between endive halves.

In a bowl, mix together oil, garlic, lemon peel, lemon juice and basil. Pour over vegetables. Broil 3 to 4 minutes. Sprinkle with cheese and return to broiler 2 to 3 minutes or until cheese is lightly browned.

Makes 4 servings.

——OLIVE & TOMATO SALAD——

1-1/2 pounds mixed yellow and green zucchini
1 tablespoon olive oil
3/4 cup halved cherry tomatoes
1/3 cup chopped pitted ripe olives
1 small head oak leaf lettuce
1 tablespoon pine nuts, toasted
GARLIC DRESSING:
3 tablespoons olive oil
1 teaspoon balsamic vinegar
1/2 garlic clove, crushed
1/2 teaspoon chopped fresh thyme
Salt and pepper

Preheat oven to 425F (220C). Wash and trim zucchini and cut into 1-inch slices. Into a roasting pan, place zucchini. Toss with oil. Bake on top rack 20 minutes or until tender.

In a large bowl, place tomatoes and olives. Stir in cooked zucchini. In a small bowl, blend dressing ingredients together. Add to bowl and stir well. Leave until zucchini are cool. Rinse and trim lettuce, discarding tough outer leaves. Tear into bite-size pieces. Arrange lettuce on 4 serving plates. Spoon zucchini mixture over lettuce. Sprinkle pine nuts over. Serve at once.

Makes 4 servings.

LETTUCE & EGG SALAD

12 quail eggs or 3 chicken eggs
6 leaf lettuce hearts
3 cups watercress
3 green onions
1 ounce Parmesan cheese or vegetarian Cheddar cheese
1/2 cup coarsely shredded chervil
DRESSING:
3 tablespoons virgin olive oil
2 teaspoons Champagne vinegar
Salt and pepper

Simmer quail eggs 3 minutes or chicken eggs 12 minutes, then cool immediately in cold water. Peel and cut into halves or quarters.

Cut each lettuce head into quarters. Discard any thick stems from the watercress. Thinly slice the green onions. Divide lettuce quarters, watercress and onions among 4 serving plate. Using a vegetable peeler, shave a little Parmesan cheese or Cheddar cheese over each. Sprinkle with chervil. Garnish each salad with cooked eggs.

In a small bowl, blend dressing ingredients together until combined. Pour over salads and serve at once.

Makes 4 servings.

—VEGETARIAN CAESAR SALAD—

2 tablespoons mayonnaise
1 tablespoon vodka
1 tablespoon lime juice
1 teaspoon Worcestershire sauce or 2 drops hot pepper
   sauce
2/3 cup light olive oil
1 tablespoon chopped fresh mint
1 tablespoon chopped fresh parsley
1/2 teaspoon ground cumin
1/4 teaspoon chili powder
1 small garlic clove, crushed
2 (1/2-inch) slices day-old bread
2 romaine lettuce heads
3/4 cup shredded vegetarian Cheddar cheese

Preheat oven to 375F (190C). In a small
bowl, blend mayonnaise, vodka, lime juice,
Worcestershire sauce or hot-pepper sauce
together. Beat in 1/3 cup of the oil, a little at
a time, until thickened slightly. Stir in half
the herbs; set aside. Mix remaining oil,
herbs, spices and garlic together. Brush over
both sides of bread. Place on a wire rack.
Bake 10 to 12 minutes. Turn bread and bake
10 to 12 minutes longer until crisp and golden
on both sides. Cool slightly, then cut into
cubes.

Just before serving, rinse lettuce, discarding
outer leaves. Dry well. In a large bowl, place
lettuce leaves. Stir in croutons and cheese.
Add dressing and toss well until evenly
coated. Serve at once.

Makes 4 servings.

──SESAME-DRESSED ENDIVE──

GINGER DRESSING:
1/3 cup light olive oil
1/2 teaspoon sesame oil
2 teaspoons orange juice
1 teaspoon balsamic vinegar
1 teaspoon grated peeled gingerroot
1/2 teaspoon grated orange peel
1/2 teaspoon honey
Salt and pepper
SALAD:
6 heads Belgian endive, halved
4 ounces green beans
1 tablespoons sesame seeds, toasted

To prepare dressing, in a screw-top jar, place all ingredients. Shake vigorously. Refrigerate to let flavors develop. Preheat broiler.

Rinse and dry endives; brush with a little dressing. Broil 3 to 4 minutes on each side until leaves become lightly charred. Meanwhile, blanch beans in boiling water 1 to 2 minutes or until crisp-tender. Drain beans, refresh under cold water and pat dry. Arrange 3 endive halves on each plate. Add beans. Drizzle with dressing and sprinkle with the sesame seeds. Serve at once.

Makes 4 servings.

—ORIENTAL CARROT SALAD—

3/4 pounds carrots
3 tablespoons peanut oil
1/2 teaspoon sesame oil
1 teaspoon grated peeled gingerroot
1 small garlic clove, sliced
1 dried red chile, seeded and crushed
2 tablespoons lemon juice
1 teaspoon sugar
1/3 cup peanuts, toasted and chopped
Salt and pepper
Cilantro leaves, to garnish

Into a large bowl, finely grate carrot.

In a skillet, heat 1 tablespoon of the peanut oil and the sesame oil. Add gingerroot, garlic and chile; cook until just turning golden. Beat in remaining oil, lemon juice and sugar. Remove from heat.

Pour dressing over carrots. Add nuts and toss well until evenly combined. Cover and let marinate 30 minutes. Stir again, season to taste and serve garnished with cilantro leaves.

Makes 4 servings.

—WILD & BROWN RICE SALAD—

1 cup wild rice
1-1/4 cups brown rice
2/3 cup pecans
6 green onions, trimmed
1/3 cup dried cherries, cranberries or raisins
2 tablespoons chopped fresh cilantro
1 tablespoon chopped fresh parsley
DRESSING:
1/2 cup olive oil
2 teaspoons raspberry vinegar
1/4 teaspoon honey or sugar
Salt and pepper

In a pan of lightly salted boiling water, cook wild rice 35 to 40 minutes or until just tender. In another pan of lightly salted boiling water, cook brown rice 25 minutes or until just tender. Drain well. Place both rices in a large bowl.

Preheat oven to 400F (205C). Roast pecans 5 to 6 minutes or until browned. Cool and coarsely chop. Set aside. Chop green onions. Add to rice with cherries and herbs. Stir well. Blend the dressing ingredients well together. Pour over salad, stir once, cover and let rice cool. Just before serving, toss in pecans and season with salt and pepper.

Makes 4 to 6 servings.

BEET & BEAN SALAD

1/4 cup hazelnuts
3/4 pound cooked beets, peeled
4 ounces green beans
2 small leeks
1 pear
1 cup cooked dried white beans
DRESSING:
2 tablespoons chopped fresh dill
1 garlic clove
1 teaspoon whole-grain mustard
1 teaspoon sherry vinegar
1/3 cup olive oil

Preheat oven to 400F (205C). Roast hazelnuts 6 to 8 minutes or until golden. Cool slightly, then chop and set aside. Cut beets into bite-size pieces. Place in a large bowl. Blanch green beans in boiling water 1 to 2 minutes until tender. Drain, refresh under cold water and pat dry. Rinse and thinly slice leeks, then quarter, core and slice pear. Add to beets with green beans and dried beans.

Prepare Dressing: In a small bowl, mix dill, garlic, mustard and vinegar together. Beat in the oil. Pour over salad, toss well and set aside 1 hour for flavors to mingle. Sprinkle hazelnuts over salad and serve at once.

Makes 4 to 6 servings.

Note: Use canned dried cannelloni or navy beans and drain well before use.

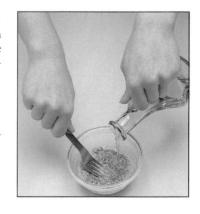

MEDITERRANEAN POTATO SALAD

1 pound new potatoes
4 ounces green beans
1 fennel bulb
1/4 cup pitted ripe olives
2 tablespoons capers, drained
2 tablespoons snipped fresh chives
2 teaspoon chopped fresh tarragon
1/4 cup virgin olive oil
Juice of 1/2 lemon
2 eggs
1 (14-oz.) can artichoke hearts, drained and halved

In a pan of lightly salted boiling water, cook potatoes 10 to 12 minutes or until just tender. Drain and place in a large bowl. Blanch beans in boiling water 1 to 2 minutes or until just tender. Drain and refresh under cold water. Pat dry. Very thinly slice fennel and halve olives. Add to potatoes with beans, capers and herbs. Stir in oil and lemon juice. Set aside until potatoes are cool.

Meanwhile, hard cook eggs. Plunge into cold water, then peel. Rough chop and add to salad with the artichoke hearts. Toss well and serve at once.

Makes 4 to 6 servings.

PANZANELLA SALAD

8 thick slices day-old Italian bread
10 plum tomatoes
1/2 small cucumber
1/2 small red onion
1/2 cup pitted ripe olives
2 tablespoons chopped fresh basil
Grated peel of 1 lemon
1/4 cup virgin olive oil
2 teaspoons balsamic vinegar
Salt and pepper
Lemon slices and basil sprigs, to garnish

Cut bread into small cubes. Place into a shallow dish. Pour over enough water to lightly moisten. Set aside 30 minutes.

Squeeze out all excess water and crumble bread into a large bowl. Cut tomatoes, cucumber, onion and olives into small pieces. Add to bread with basil and lemon peel. Stir well.

In a small bowl, heat oil and vinegar together. Pour over salad. Season with salt and pepper; toss salad until evenly combined. Cover and refrigerate at least 30 minutes; bring salad to room temperature before serving. Garnish with lemon slices and basil sprigs.

Makes 4 to 6 servings.

——————EGGPLANT SALAD——————

1 small eggplant
3 tablespoons olive oil
4 ounces shiitake mushrooms
1 pound mixed salad greens
1-1/2 tablespoons chopped fresh cilantro
1/4 cup hazelnuts, toasted and coarsely chopped
DRESSING:
1/3 cup olive oil
1 teaspoon sesame oil
2 teaspoons light soy sauce
1 tablespoon balsamic vinegar
1/2 teaspoon sugar
Pepper

Preheat broiler. Cut eggplant into thin slices. Brush slices with a little oil; broil 2 to 3 minutes on each side or until charred and softened. Let cool. Thinly slice mushrooms. In a small skillet, heat remaining oil. Stir-fry mushrooms over medium heat 3 to 4 minutes or until tender. Drain on paper towels until cool.

Rinse salad greens, shake off all excess water and place into a large bowl. Sprinkle with cilantro and nuts. In a small bowl, blend all dressing ingredients together until well mixed. Add the eggplant and mushrooms to salad. Pour dressing over salad, toss well and serve at once.

Makes 4 servings.

── TOMATO & PEACH SALAD ──

1/4 cup coarsely shredded basil leaves
1 garlic clove, chopped
1 tablespoon pine nuts, toasted
3 tablespoons virgin olive oil
1 tablespoon freshly grated Parmesan or vegetarian
   Cheddar cheese
1/2 cup reduced-calorie mayonnaise
Salt and pepper
2 large beefsteak tomatoes
2 large ripe peaches
1/2 small red onion (optional)
Grated peel of 1 lemon
Basil leaves, to garnish

In a spice grinder or food processor, puree basil, garlic and pine nuts until fairly smooth. Blend in 2 tablespoons of the oil and transfer to a small bowl. Stir in cheese, mayonnaise, salt and pepper. Cover and refrigerate until required.

Thinly slice tomatoes. Pit peaches and cut into thin wedges. Thinly slice onion, if using. Arrange tomatoes and peaches in rings on a large platter. Sprinkle with onion and grated lemon peel. Spoon basil dressing into center of salad. Drizzle remaining oil over tomatoes. Serve garnished with a few basil leaves.

Makes 4 servings.

PEA TABBOULEH

1-1/4 cups bulgur wheat
2/3 cup olive oil
1 garlic clove, crushed
1 tablespoon red-wine vinegar
1 tablespoon chopped fresh cilantro
1 tablespoon chopped fresh mint
1 teaspoon ground coriander
1/2 teaspoon ground cumin
4 ounces sugarsnap peas
1 cup frozen green peas, thawed
1 large ripe peach, chopped
1 red onion, finely chopped
Salt and pepper

In a large bowl, cover bulgur wheat with plenty of cold water. Let soak 30 minutes. Drain well and squeeze out excess liquid. In a small bowl, mix together oil, garlic, vinegar, herbs and spices. Pour over bulgur wheat. Stir well, cover and set aside 30 minutes.

In a pan of boiling water, cook sugarsnap peas 2 minutes and green peas 1 minute. Drain both and refresh under cold water. Pat all peas dry. Stir into bulgur wheat with the peach, onion, salt and pepper.

Makes 4 to 6 servings.

WARM PASTA SALAD

1/2 pound mixed fresh mushrooms
1/4 cup drained sun-dried tomatoes in oil, sliced
1/2 cup olive oil
2 garlic cloves, chopped
Grated peel of 1 lemon
1 tablespoon lemon juice
2 tablespoons chopped fresh mint
2-1/2 cups dried penne
2 tomatoes, chopped
Salt and pepper

Thinly slice mushrooms. Into a large bowl, place mushrooms with sun-dried tomatoes.

In a skillet, heat 1 tablespoon of the oil. Add garlic; cook 1 minute until starting to turn golden. Remove pan from heat and stir in remaining oil, lemon peel, lemon juice and mint. Pour half over mushrooms and reserve the remainder. Stir mushrooms until well coated. Cover and refrigerate several hours to soften.

In a pan of lightly salted boiling water, cook pasta 10 minutes or until tender but firm to the bite. Drain well. Toss pasta with remaining dressing and stir into marinated mushrooms with tomatoes. Season with salt and pepper.

Makes 4 servings.

Note: Use a selection of button, oyster and shiitake mushrooms.

—SPINACH & CHEESE SALAD—

1/2 cup olive oil
3 shallots, thinly sliced
1 tablespoon red-wine vinegar
1 tablespoon dry red wine
1/2 teaspoon sugar
1/2 pound young spinach leaves
4 thick slices French bread
1 garlic clove, halved
4 ounces goat cheese, sliced
2 tablespoons pine nuts, toasted

Preheat oven to 375F (190C). In a small pan, heat 1 tablespoon of the oil. Add shallots; cook 3 to 4 minutes or until light golden.

Add vinegar, wine and sugar. Simmer 5 minutes. Strain shallots into a bowl, reserving liquid and shallots. Rinse spinach leaves. Shake off excess water, place in a plastic bag and refrigerate 1 hour to crisp. Meanwhile, place sliced bread onto a baking sheet. Bake 5 minutes. Rub crisp sides all over with garlic. Turn over and cook 5 minutes longer to crisp other sides. Rub with garlic and return to oven 5 to 6 minutes longer or until bread is completely crisp. Let cool.

Place spinach leaves into a bowl. Toss in shallots. Whisk remaining oil into shallot liquid and pour all but 1 tablespoon over salad. Transfer to plates. Place a cheese slice on top of each bread slice; broil 3 to 4 minutes or until melted and browned. Place in center of each plate. Drizzle reserved dressing over cheese and sprinkle with pine nuts. Serve at once.

Makes 4 servings.

- WATERCRESS & CHEESE SALAD -

3 cups watercress leaves
3 cups arugula leaves
1 pear, quartered and sliced
1 tablespoon pumpkin seeds, toasted
3/4 cup crumbled gorgonzola cheese
DRESSING:
3 tablespoons olive oil
1/2 teaspoon balsamic vinegar
1 teaspoon whole-grain mustard
1 tablespoon chopped fresh mint
Salt and pepper

Rinse and dry watercress and arugula, shaking off excess water. Transfer to a large bowl. Stir in the sliced pear, pumpkin seeds and cheese.

In a bowl, beat all dressing ingredients together until blended. Pour over salad, toss well and serve at once.

Makes 4 servings.

NIÇOISE PLATTER

8 large asparagus spears
4 ounces green beans
2 carrots carrots
6 ounces celeriac, peeled
4 ounces cooked beets, peeled
1 (15-oz.) can dried navy beans
8 tablespoons olive oil
4 tablespoons lemon juice
Salt and pepper
2 garlic cloves, crushed
1 teaspoon each red wine and raspberry vinegar
1 tablespoon chopped almonds, toasted
Snipped fresh chives and chopped fresh parsley
1 teaspoon whole-grain mustard
1 teaspoon creamed horseradish
8 marinated artichokes from a jar, halved

Peel asparagus almost to tips. Cook in boiling salted water 3 minutes or until just tender. Drain, refresh and pat dry. Cook green beans 2 minutes or until tender. Drain, refresh and pat dry. Finely grate carrot and celeriac. Dice beets. Drain and rinse navy beans. Marinate asparagus in 1 tablespoon of the oil, the lemon juice, salt and pepper 1 hour. Marinate green beans in 1 tablespoon of the oil, half of the garlic, wine vinegar, salt and pepper 1 hour.

In a bowl, mix carrots with 2 tablespoons of the oil, the raspberry vinegar, almonds and chives. In a bowl, mix celeriac with 1 tablespoon of the oil, the mustard, 1 tablespoon lemon juice, salt and pepper. In a bowl, mix beets with creamed horseradish and 1 tablespoon of the oil. In a bowl, mix navy beans with 2 tablespoons of the oil, remaining lemon juice, remaining garlic, parsley, salt and pepper. Arrange all the vegetables on a large platter and serve.

Makes 8 servings.

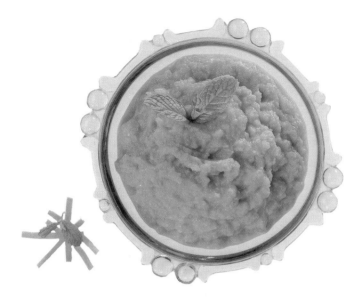

──PUREED GINGER CARROTS──

2-1/2 pounds carrots
2/3 cup vegetable stock (page 65)
2 tablespoons hazelnut oil
1 large onion, chopped
1 garlic clove, chopped
2 teaspoons grated peeled gingerroot
1 teaspoon ground cumin
Pinch of freshly grated nutmeg
Palt and pepper
Mint sprigs, to garnish

Roughly chop carrots. In a large pan, place carrots with stock. Slowly bring to a boil. Reduce heat, cover and simmer 20 minutes until or carrots are tender.

In a skillet, heat 1 tablespoon of the oil. Add onion, garlic, gingerroot and cumin; cook 5 minutes or until soft. Transfer to a blender or food processor. Add cooked carrots and stock. Puree until smooth. Pass through a food mill or fine strainer if the puree is not completely smooth.

Beat in remaining oil, freshly grated nutmeg, salt and pepper to taste. Serve hot, garnished with mint.

Makes 6 servings.

Note: This puree can easily be made ahead of time. To reheat, place in baking dish, cover with foil and bake 20 minutes at 400F (205C). Or, cover with vented plastic wrap and microwave on MEDIUM 6 to 8 minutes or until hot.

–CREAMY FENNEL & LEEK BAKE–

3 medium-size fennel bulbs
2 leeks, trimmed and rinsed
3/4 cup fromage frais or half and half
1/2 cup shredded Cheddar cheese
1/4 teaspoon freshly grated nutmeg
Salt and pepper
1 garlic clove, halved
1/4 cup freshly grated Parmesan cheese
1/2 cup fresh bread crumbs
Butter (optional)

Preheat oven to 400F (205C). Trim fennel, discarding any discolored outer leaves, reserving a few leaves for garnishing. Slice fennel thinly.

Slice leeks. Into a large bowl, place leeks with fennel. Stir in fromage frais, Cheddar cheese, nutmeg, salt and pepper. Stir well until evenly combined.

Rub inside of a shallow flameproof dish with the garlic. Spoon in fennel mixture, smoothing the surface. Combine Parmesan cheese and bread crumbs and sprinkle over surface of dish. Dot with a little butter, if desired. Cover loosely with foil and bake 1 hour or until fennel is tender. Remove foil and bake 10 minutes longer to brown, or broil until browned. Garnish with reserved fennel.

Makes 6 to 8 servings.

— GARLIC-ROASTED POTATOES —

2-1/4 pounds new potatoes
12 unpeeled shallots
12 unpeeled garlic cloves
1 tablespoon chopped fresh sage
1 tablespoon chopped fresh thyme or rosemary
1/4 cup hazelnut oil or olive oil
Salt and pepper

Preheat oven to 400F (205C). Rinse and dry potatoes and halve any large ones. Trim shallots, removing root ends. Combine with potatoes, garlic and herbs.

Into a roasting pan, place oil. Place in the oven 5 minutes until hot and starting to smoke. Add potato and shallot mixture, taking care not to splash the hot oil. Stir until potatoes, shallots, garlic and herbs are well coated.

Return to the oven and roast 50 to 60 minutes or until potatoes are tender, turning occasionally to brown evenly. Transfer to a hot serving dish and serve at once.

Makes 6 servings.

—— BROCCOLI & TOMATOES ——

2-1/4 pounds tomatoes
3 tablespoons olive oil
1 garlic clove, crushed
2 teaspoons lemon juice
1 teaspoon hot pepper sauce
1 teaspoon balsamic vinegar
1 pound broccoli
1/4 cup sliced pitted ripe olives
1/4 cup pine nuts, toasted
1 tablespoon chopped fresh parsley
1/4 cup Parmesan shavings

Into a large heatproof bowl, place tomatoes. Pour boiling water over to cover.

Leave 1 minute, then drain. Refresh under cold water and pat dry. Peel and discard skins and seeds and finely chop flesh. In a large saucepan, heat oil. Add tomatoes, garlic, lemon juice, hot pepper sauce and vinegar. Bring to a boil, cover and cook 10 minutes. Uncover, increase heat and cook until slightly reduced and thickened.

Meanwhile, cut broccoli into flowerets. Steam 5 minutes. Add to sauce with olives, nuts and parsley and stir until combined. Transfer to a warmed serving dish. Sprinkle with Parmesan shavings and serve at once.

Makes 4 servings.

Note: For vegans, omit Parmesan cheese.

— BEETS WITH HORSERADISH —

14 to 18 small beets
1/2 cup plain yogurt
2 tablespoons mayonnaise
2 tablespoons snipped fresh chives
2 teaspoons grated horseradish (preferably fresh)
1/2 teaspoon whole-grain mustard
Salt and pepper
Chives, to garnish

Preheat oven to 350F (175C). Carefully rinse beets to remove any dirt. Trim stems to about 2 inches. Dry well.

In a small roasting pan, place beets. Cover loosely with foil and bake 2-1/4 hours or until skins wrinkle to the touch and beets are tender.

Meanwhile, in a small bowl, mix all remaining ingredients together. Adjust seasoning and refrigerate 2 hours. Cool cooked beets a few minutes and peel away skins. Serve at once with horseradish cream, garnished with chives.

Makes 6 servings.

──SWEET POTATO WEDGES──

About 2 tablespoons olive oil
4 small sweet potatoes (1-1/2 pounds)
2 teaspoons paprika
1/2 teaspoon chili powder
Salt and pepper
Thyme sprigs, to garnish

Preheat oven to 450F (230C). Pour enough olive oil into a large roasting pan to just cover bottom. Place in the oven 2 to 3 minutes or until hot.

Rinse and dry potatoes. Cut each one into 8 wedges. Carefully spoon into hot oil, avoiding splashing. Bake on top rack 10 minutes, then turn potatoes over and bake 10 minutes longer until golden on outside and cooked through.

Mix spices together. Using a slotted spoon, transfer potatoes to a serving dish. Sprinkle with spices, salt and pepper and stir well to coat evenly. Serve hot, garnished with thyme.

Makes 6 servings.

—————— SAUCY BUTTER BEANS ——————

1 cup dried butter beans or pinto beans, soaked
   overnight in cold water to cover
1 bay leaf
About 1/4 cup virgin olive oil
1 red onion, chopped
2 garlic cloves, chopped
1 tablespoon chopped fresh sage
1 pound tomatoes
1 teaspoon balsamic vinegar
Salt and pepper
1 tablespoon chopped fresh parsley

Drain beans. In a pan, place beans with bay leaf and enough fresh cold water to cover. Boil 10 minutes.

Reduce heat and simmer, covered, 40 to 45 minutes, or until tender. In a large pan, heat 1/4 cup oil. Add onion, garlic and sage; cook 10 minutes or until softened. Peel and seed tomatoes. Chop flesh and add to pan with vinegar. Cover and cook 5 minutes or until softened.

Drain cooked beans. Rinse well and shake off excess water. Stir into onion mixture in pan. Cover and cook 4 to 5 minutes or until heated through. Season to taste and sprinkle with chopped parsley. Serve with extra olive oil drizzled over beans.

Makes 4 servings.

Note: This dish is delicious served warm or cool. Pass around plenty of crusty bread to soak up juices.

—SUMMER VEGETABLE MEDLEY —

1/2 pound baby new potatoes, scrubbed
1 small fennel bulb, trimmed
4 ounces baby carrots
2 ounces baby corn-on-the-cob
2 ounces asparagus spears
2 baby leeks, trimmed
4 green onions, trimmed
2 tablespoons olive oil
1 cup vegetable stock (page 65)
Grated peel and juice of 1 lime
1/2 teaspoon coriander seeds, brusied
2 bay leaves
2 sprigs each parsley and cilantro
2 tablespoons each sherry and wine vinegar
1-1/2 teaspoons sugar
4 tomatoes, into wedges

In a pan of boiling water, cook potatoes 5 minutes. Drain and set aside. Thickly slice fennel. Trim carrots, corn and asparagus. Thickly slice leeks and onions. In a large pan, heat oil. Add fennel, carrots and corn; cook over low heat 5 minutes. Add asparagus, leeks, onions and potatoes and cook 2 minutes. Add all remaining ingredients to pan, except the tomatoes. Bring to a boil, cover and simmer 6 to 8 minutes until all vegetables are crisp-tender.

Into a clean pan, strain stock. Transfer vegetables to a large dish. Bring stock to a boil. Stir in tomatoes and simmer 3 minutes. Pour mixture over vegetables and let cool. Cover and refrigerate several hours or overnight. Let return to room temperature and discard herbs before serving.

Makes 4 servings.

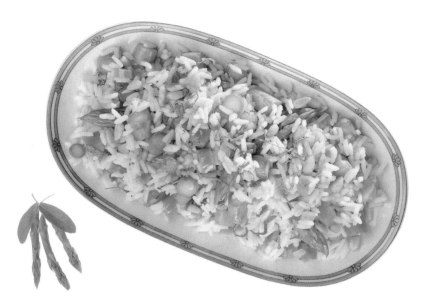

RICE WITH ASPARAGUS & NUTS

4 tablespoons butter or margarine
1 small onion, finely chopped
1 garlic clove, crushed
1-1/4 cups long-grain rice
2 cups vegetable stock (page 65)
1/2 pound asparagus spears, trimmed
3 tablespoons pine nuts
2 tablespoons chopped fresh sage
Salt and pepper

In a saucepan melt 1 tablespoon of the butter. Add onion and garlic; cook 5 minutes. Add rice and stir-fry 1 minute or until transparent and glossy. Pour in stock. Bring to a boil, stir once, cover and simmer 12 minutes.

Steam asparagus 3 minutes. Refresh under cold water, then drain and dry well. Coarsely chop. In a large pan, melt remaining butter. Add pine nuts; stir-fry over medium heat 3 to 4 minutes or until golden. Add sage and asparagus. Stir in cooked rice. Season with salt and pepper and heat through, stirring, 2 minutes. Serve at once.

Makes 6 servings.

Note: For vegans, replace butter with 4 tablespoons olive oil.

MASHED JERUSALEM ARTICHOKES

3/4 pound Jerusalem artichokes, scrubbed
1/2 pound red potatoes, scrubbed
2 tablespoons hazelnut oil
1 tablespoon chopped fresh tarragon
2 teaspoons whole-grain mustard
Salt and pepper

Preheat oven to 400F (205C). Cut away any knobbly bits from artichokes and cut any large ones in half.

Cut potatoes into similar-size pieces. In a roasting pan, place artichokes and potatoes. Toss with 1 tablespoon of the oil. Bake 35 to 40 minutes or until artichokes and potatoes are tender.

Pass through a food mill or mash well. Stir in remaining oil, tarragon and mustard. Season with salt and pepper and serve hot.

Makes 4 servings.

——————— THREE PEAS & BEANS ———————

1 tablespoon olive oil
1 leek, trimmed and sliced
4 ounces thin green beans, trimmed
4 ounces sugarsnap peas, trimmed
3 tablespoons vegetable stock (page 65)
1/2 teaspoon sugar
4 ounces snow peas, trimmed
1 cup green peas, thawed if frozen
Grated peel and juice of 1/2 lemon
1 tablespoon chopped fresh mint
1 tablespoon snipped fresh chives
1 tablespoon butter or margarine
Salt and pepper

In a large pan, heat oil. Add leek; cook 2 minutes. Add beans and sugarsnap peas and stir-fry 1 minute. Add stock and sugar, cover and simmer 2 minutes.

Add snow peas and green peas to pan. Cover and cook 2 minutes longer. Remove from heat and stir in lemon peel, lemon juice, herbs, butter, salt and pepper. Serve hot.

Makes 4 servings.

Note: For vegans, replace butter with 1 tablespoon olive oil.

CREAMED BEANS

1-1/2 pounds fava beans, peeled and outer shell
  removed
2 tablespoons olive oil
1 leek, trimmed and thinly sliced
1/3 cup vegetable stock (page 65)
1 tablespoon chopped fresh parsley
2 teaspoons chopped fresh tarragon
1/3 cup lowfat cream cheese
1/4 cup grated Parmesan cheese or vegetarian Cheddar
  cheese
Salt and pepper
Toasted bread triangles, to serve
Parsley sprigs, to garnish

Preheat oven to 400F (205C). Rinse beans
and pat dry. In a large pan, heat 1 tablespoon
of the oil. Add leek; cook 5 minutes or until
softened. Add beans and stir-fry 2 minutes.
Add stock; simmer, uncovered, 3 minutes. In
a blender or food processor, puree drained
beans with herbs and cream cheese, salt and
pepper until smooth. Transfer to a shallow
flameproof dish and level the surface.

Sprinkle with Parmesan cheese. Drizzle with
remaining olive oil. Bake 10 minutes or until
bubbling. Brown under a broiler. Arrange
triangles of toasted bread around dish.
Garnish with parsley sprigs and serve hot.

Makes 6 servings.

Note: If possible, use fresh fava beans. You
will need approximately double the amount
of beans in the pods. Alternatively, use
frozen beans and thaw before using.

— BARLEY WITH VERMICELLI —

1/4 cup butter or margarine
1 red onion, thinly sliced
1/2 red bell pepper, thinly sliced
2 large tomatoes, peeled, seeded and diced
2/3 cup pearl barley
2 ounces dried vermicelli
2 cups vegetable stock (page 65)
1 tablespoon chopped fresh parsley
Salt and black pepper

Preheat oven to 400F (205C). In a large flameproof casserole dish, melt butter. Add onion and bell pepper; cook 3 minutes. Stir in tomatoes and simmer 2 minutes longer.

Rinse the barley with cold water. Drain thoroughly and stir into pan. Add vermicelli, breaking it into short pieces as you go. Stir-fry 2 minutes. Add stock and parsley. Cover with foil and bake 50 to 60 minutes or until all liquid is absorbed and the barley is tender. Season with salt and black pepper and serve with a crisp green salad.

Makes 4 servings.

BUTTERY COUSCOUS

2 cups couscous
1-1/3 cups green lima beans
1 (8-oz.) can whole-kernel corn, drained
1 cup green peas
1/2 cup butter or margarine
1 teaspoon ground cumin
1 teaspoon ground paprika
1 tablespoon chopped fresh cilantro
1/4 cup chopped mixed nuts, toasted
Juice of 1/2 lime
Salt and pepper
Lime slices and parsley, to garnish

Rinse couscous until all grains are moistened; set aside to soak 5 minutes. Stir grains with a fork to separate. Steam 12 to 15 minutes or until tender. In a pan of boiling water, blanch beans 2 minutes. Drain and dry well. Blanch corn 2 minutes and peas 1 minute. Drain and dry well.

In a large pan, melt butter. Stir in spices and cook over low heat 2 minutes. Add blanched vegetables and cook 2 minutes longer. Fluff cooked couscous with a fork to break up any lumps. Stir into pan until well coated with butter. Stir in cilantro, nuts, lime juice, salt and pepper. Serve hot. Garnish with lime slices and parsley.

Makes 4 to 6 servings.

—CAULIFLOWER & COCONUT—

1 cauliflower
2 tablespoons light olive oil
1 teaspoon sesame oil
1 red chile, seeded and sliced
1 (1/2-inch) piece gingerroot, finely chopped
2 shallots, thinly sliced
1/3 cup shredded coconut
1 tablespoon light soy sauce
1 teaspoon sherry vinegar

Trim and discard cauliflower leaves and cut out central core. Cut flowerets into bite-size pieces. Steam 5 to 6 minutes or until crisp-tender.

Meanwhile, in a nonstick skillet, heat 1 tablespoon of the olive oil and the sesame oil. Add chile, gingerroot and shallots; cook 5 minutes or until softened.

Add coconut. Stir-fry over medium heat 3 to 4 minutes or until golden. Stir in cauliflower, remaining oil, soy sauce and vinegar. Serve hot or warm.

Makes 4 servings.

HERBED LENTILS

1-1/4 cups lentils, soaked overnight in cold water to
    cover
1/3 cup olive oil
2 shallots, finely chopped
2 garlic cloves, crushed
1-1/2 tablespoons chopped fresh mint
1-1/2 tablespoons chopped fresh tarragon
1 tablespoon balsamic vinegar
Salt and pepper
Cucumber salad, to serve (optional)

Drain soaked lentils. In a large saucepan, place lentils. Cover with fresh cold water. Bring to a boil, cover and simmer 35 to 40 minutes or until lentils are tender. Drain well.

In a large pan, heat oil. Add shallots and garlic; cook 5 minutes. Stir in mint, tarragon, lentils and vinegar. Simmer 5 minutes. Season with salt and pepper and serve hot or cool. Serve with a cucumber salad, if desired.

Makes 6 to 8 servings.

— MUSHROOM RATATOUILLE —

1/2 ounce dried cep mushrooms
2/3 cup boiling water
1 (14-oz.) can chopped tomatoes
3 tablespoons olive oil
1 garlic clove, crushed
1 tablespoon chopped fresh basil
1 large onion, chopped
2 teaspoons chopped fresh thyme
14 ounces mixed fresh mushrooms
Salt and pepper
Basil leaves, to garnish

In a heatproof bowl, place dried mushrooms. Add boiling water; soak 20 minutes. Strain, reserving liquid. Chop mushrooms.

In a pan, place tomatoes, 1 tablespoon of the oil, the garlic and basil. Bring to a boil, then simmer 20 minutes.

In a large skillet, heat remaining oil. Add onion and thyme; cook 5 minutes. Add dried and fresh mushrooms and stir-fry over high heat 3 to 4 minutes or until tender. Add soaking liquid and simmer 3 minutes. Stir in tomato sauce and simmer 5 minutes. Season with salt and pepper and serve hot, warm or cool. Garnish with basil.

Makes 4 to 6 servings.

– MOCHA ESPRESSO ICE CREAM –

2 cups milk
2/3 cup whipping cream
1/3 cup medium-ground espresso coffee beans
3 ounces semisweet chocolate, chopped
6 egg yolks
3/4 cup sugar
Chocolate shavings, to decorate

Into a small saucepan, place milk, cream, ground coffee and 2 ounces of the chocolate. Heat slowly until almost boiling. Remove from heat and set aside 30 minutes for the flavors to infuse.

In a large bowl, beat egg yolks and sugar together until thick and pale. Gradually beat in mocha mixture and transfer to a clean saucepan. Heat gently, stirring, until mixture thickens, but do not boil. Refrigerate until chilled.

Transfer mixture to a freezerproof container and freeze. Beat to mix and break up ice crystals after about 1 hour and again at hourly intervals until almost firm. Stir in remaining chocolate, cover and let freeze completely. Remove from freezer 20 minutes before serving to soften. Decorate with chocolate shavings.

Makes 4 servings.

–WHOLE-WHEAT NUT BISCOTTI–

2 eggs
1/3 cup sugar
1-3/4 cups whole-wheat flour
1-1/2 teaspoons baking powder
Pinch of salt
1 tablespoon light olive oil
3/4 cup Brazil nuts, toasted and ground
1/2 teaspoon caraway seeds
1/2 teaspoon freshly grated lemon peel

Preheat oven to 350F (175C). Lightly grease a baking sheet. Beat eggs and sugar together until very thick and pale.

Beat in flour, baking powder and salt to form a soft, sticky dough. Stir in remaining ingredients. Turn out onto a clean surface. Divide dough in half and roll into 2 logs about 8 inches long. Transfer to prepared baking sheet. Bake 20 minutes. Remove from oven and increase oven temperature to 400F (205C).

Using a serrated knife, cut logs into 1/2-inch cookies, slicing diagonally. Place cookies, cut-sides down, on the baking sheet. Bake 8 to 10 minutes or until browned around edges. Cool on a wire rack.

Makes 32 cookies.

Note: Sprinkle the cookies with a little confectioners' sugar, if desired.

——LEMON-POPPY SEED CAKE——

4 eggs, separated
1/2 cup sugar
Grated peel and juice of 1 lemon
3/4 cup blanched, finely ground almonds
3/4 cup dried bread crumbs
1 tablespoon poppy seeds
2 tablespoons brandy
Mint leaves and lemon peel, to decorate
RASPBERRY SAUCE:
1/2 pound fresh raspberries
1 tablespoon honey
1/2 teaspoon ground cinnamon

Preheat oven to 350F (175C). Grease and line the bottom of an 8-inch springform pan with waxed paper. In a large bowl, beat egg yolks, sugar, lemon peel and lemon juice together until pale and creamy. In another bowl, beat egg whites until stiff. Fold in with almonds, bread crumbs and poppy seeds until evenly combined. Transfer to prepared pan. Bake 40 minutes or until golden and firm to the touch. Remove from oven and stab all over with a wooden pick. Pour brandy over cake and let cool.

Make sauce: Reserve 12 raspberries for decoration. In a blender or food processor, puree remaining raspberries until smooth. Pass through a fine strainer to remove seeds. Beat in honey and cinnamon. Serve cake cut into wedges, topped with the sauce. Decorate with reserved raspberries, mint and lemon peel.

Makes 6 servings.

Note: Frozen raspberries can be substituted for fresh.

-FIGS WITH CINNAMON CREAM-

9 large ripe figs
1/4 cup unsalted butter
4 teaspoons brandy
1 tablespoon brown sugar
Almond slices, to decorate
CINNAMON CREAM:
2/3 cup whipping cream
1 teaspoon ground cinnamon
1 tablespoon brandy
2 teaspoons honey

Prepare Cinnamon Cream: In a small bowl, combine all ingredients. Cover and refrigerate 30 minutes to allow flavors to develop.

Preheat broiler. Halve figs and thread onto 6 skewers. In a small pan, melt butter. Stir in brandy.

Brush figs with brandy butter and sprinkle with a little sugar. Broil 4 to 5 minutes or until bubbling and golden. Whip Cinnamon Cream until just soft peaks form, decorate with almond slices and serve with broiled figs.

Makes 6 servings.

PEARS WITH CHOCOLATE SAUCE

1/2 cup ricotta cheese
1/2 cup hazelnuts, finely ground
2 tablespoons honey
2 small egg yolks
Seeds from 1 cardamom pod, crushed
4 large pears
Mint sprigs, to decorate
CHOCOLATE SAUCE:
4 ounces semisweet chocolate
3 tablespoons unsalted butter
2 tablespoons brandy
2 tablespoons dairy sour cream

In a bowl, cream together cheese, hazelnuts, honey, egg yolks and cardamon seeds.

Preheat oven to 375F (190C). Cut a thin slice from bottom of each pear. Using a corer or small spoon, carefully scoop out core as far up inside pear as possible, without damaging skin. Fill cavities with ricotta mixture, pressing in well; smooth bottoms flat. Peel pears and place in a small roasting pan. Cover with foil. Bake 45 to 50 minutes until pears are tender.

Prepare sauce: Just before pears are cooked, into a small pan, place the chocolate, butter, brandy and sour cream. Heat gently until melted, stir well and keep warm. Transfer cooked pears to serving plates. Slice in half to reveal filling and top with sauce. Serve immediately, decorated with mint.

Makes 4 servings.

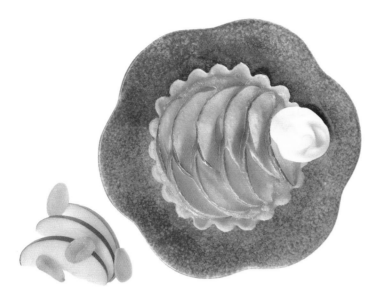

—APPLE & ALMOND TARTLETS—

Prepared pie crust dough for 2 (9-inch) crusts
1/3 cup unsalted butter, softened
1/3 cup sugar
2 eggs, beaten
1/2 cup blanched almonds, finely ground
1 teaspoon ground cinnamon
3 ounces vegetarian Cheddar cheese
3 small apples
2 tablespoons apricot jam
Whipped cream, to decorate

Divide dough into 6 pieces. On a lightly floured surface, roll out each piece to a 6-inch circle. Use to line 6 (4-inch) tartlet pans. Prick bottoms and refrigerate 30 minutes.

Preheat oven to 375F (190C); place a baking sheet on middle shelf. In a bowl, cream butter and sugar together until soft and beat in the eggs, almonds and cinnamon. Finely shred cheese and stir into mixture. Line tartlet shells with foil and pie weights. Bake blind on baking sheet 10 minutes. Remove weights and foil and bake 8 to 10 minutes longer until pastry is crisp and golden. Cool slightly, then spread cheese mixture over bottom.

Quarter and core apples and cut into thin slices. Arrange slices over cheese mixture in circles. Bake 15 minutes. Reduce oven temperature to 350F (175C). Bake 10 to 15 minutes longer until firm to the touch. In a small pan, heat jam with 1 teaspoon water until melted. Press through a fine strainer, then carefully brush over tartlets to glaze. Serve warm with whipped cream.

Makes 6 servings.

—BAKED MANGO CUSTARDS—

2 large ripe mangoes
Juice of 1 lime
4 egg yolks
1/3 cup sugar
1 teaspoon ground ginger
1/4 teaspoon ground mixed spice
2-1/2 cups whipping cream
Toasted slivered almonds, to decorate

Preheat oven to 325F (160C). Peel mangoes. Cut away and discard pits and coarsely chop the flesh. Into a blender or food processor, place mango flesh and lime juice and puree until smooth.

In a bowl, beat egg yolks, sugar and spices together until pale and thick. Stir in mango puree. Put 2 cups whipping cream into a pan and heat until simmering. Beat into mango mixture until evenly blended. Pour into 8 ramekin dishes. Place in a roasting pan and pour in enough boiling water to come two-thirds up sides of ramekins. Bake 30 minutes or until set, remove from the oven and let cool. Refrigerate several hours.

In a bowl, beat remaining cream until stiff. Spoon or pipe a swirl onto each custard and decorate with almonds.

Makes 8 servings.

EXOTIC FRUIT BRÛLÉE

3 egg yolks
1/4 cup sugar
1 teaspoon vanilla extract
2/3 cup crème fraîche
2 teaspoons kirsch or brandy
1 small ripe mango, peeled
1 small ripe pear, peeled, quartered and cored
1 large ripe fig
8 large ripe strawberries, hulled
Freshly grated nutmeg
Tuille cookies, to serve

Preheat broiler. In a bowl, beat egg yolks, sugar and vanilla together until pale and thick. Stir in crème fraîche and kirsch or brandy; set aside. Remove mango pit and cut flesh into thin slices. Slice pear, fig and strawberries thinly. Arrange all the fruit over bottoms of 4 individual gratin dishes.

Carefully pour one-quarter of the custard over each dish, as evenly as possible, to cover the fruit. Grate a little fresh nutmeg over custard. Preheat broiler. Place 4 to 6 inches from heat source; broil 3 to 4 minutes or until custard is lightly caramelized. Cool slightly and serve with tuille or other sweet cookies.

Makes 4 servings.

MELON & BERRIES

3/4 pound mixed fresh berries (raspberries,
    strawberries, blackberries, blueberries)
1/2 cup Muscat dessert wine
1 teaspoon chopped preserved stem ginger
2 teaspoons stem ginger syrup (from jar)
1 teaspoon shredded fresh mint
2 small cantaloupe melons
Mint leaves, to decorate

Rinse and dry berries; hull and halve as necessary. Arrange in a bowl. Pour wine, ginger,
ginger syrup and mint over berries. Stir well,
cover and refrigerate 2 hours.

With a sharp knife, cut melons in half,
cutting into flesh in a zigzag pattern all the
way around centers of each fruit to form
attractive edges. Carefully scoop out and
discard seeds. Fill each hollow with a large
spoonful of chilled berries. Pour in juices,
decorate with mint leaves.

Makes 4 servings.

— FRUIT & ELDERBERRY CREAM —

1/2 cup whipping cream
1/2 cup plain yogurt
2 tablespoons elderberry syrup
1 small ripe mango
1 small ripe papaya
1 large ripe peach
1 large apple
4 ounces strawberries
4 ounces bunch seedless grapes
Freshly grated nutmeg and fresh mint, to decorate

In a bowl, whip cream. Gently fold in yogurt and elderberry syrup. Cover and refrigerate until required.

Peel mango. Cut down each side of pit and cut the flesh into thin slices. Peel and halve the papaya. Scoop out and discard seeds and cut flesh into thin strips. Halve and pit peach. Cut into thin wedges. Quarter and core apple. Cut into thin wedges. Hull and halve strawberries.

Arrange all prepared fruit and the grapes on a large platter. Place bowl of elderberry cream in center. Sprinkle a little nutmeg over cream and serve the fruit decorated with the mint.

Makes 8 servings.

Note: Use any fruit liqueur as an alternative to elderberry syrup, if desired. Sprinkle apple and peach with lemon juice if not serving immediately.

INDEX